THE REVE

Former general editors
Clifford Leech
F. David Hoeniger
E. A. J. Honigmann
Eugene M. Waith

General editors
David Bevington, Richard Dutton, Alison Findlay,
J. R. Mulryne and Helen Ostovich

THE WOMAN
IN THE MOON

Manchester University Press

THE REVELS PLAYS

THE REVELS PLAYS

THE WOMAN
IN THE MOON

JOHN LYLY

edited by Leah Scragg

MANCHESTER
UNIVERSITY PRESS

Manchester and New York

*Distributed exclusively in the USA
by* Palgrave

Introduction, critical apparatus, etc. © Leah Scragg 2006

The right of Leah Scragg to be identified as the editor of this work has been asserted by her in accordance with the Copyright, Designs and Patents Act 1988.

This edition Published by Manchester University Press
Oxford Road, Manchester M13 9NR, UK
and Room 400, 175 Fifth Avenue, New York, NY 10010, USA
www.manchesteruniversitypress.co.uk

Distributed exclusively in the USA by
Palgrave, 175 Fifth Avenue, New York NY 10010, USA

Distributed exclusively in Canada by
UBC Press, University of British Columbia, 2029 West Mall,
Vancouver, BC, Canada V6T 1Z2

British Library Cataloguing-in-Publication Data
A catalogue record for this book is available from the British Library

Library of Congress Cataloging-in-Publication Data
A catalog record for this book is available from the Library of Congress

ISBN 13: 978 0 7190 7245 1

First published in hardback 2006 by Manchester University Press
This paperback edition first published 2011

Printed by Lightning Source

Katharine Hepburn in the role of Pandora (Bryn Mawr
College, 1928). Courtesy of The Academy of Motion Picture
Arts and Sciences (Beverly Hills), reproduced by kind per-
mission of Katharine Houghton.

Contents

General Editors' Preface

Clifford Leech conceived of the Revels Plays as a series in the mid-1950s, modelling the project on the New Arden Shakespeare. The aim, as he wrote in 1958, was 'to apply to Shakespeare's predecessors, contemporaries and successors the methods that are now used in Shakespeare's editing'. The plays chosen were to include well-known works from the early Tudor period to about 1700, as well as others less familiar but of literary and theatrical merit: 'the plays included', Leech wrote, 'should be such as to deserve and indeed demand performance'. We owe it to Clifford Leech that the idea became reality. He set the high standards of the series, ensuring that editors of individual volumes produced work of lasting merit, equally useful for teachers and students, theatre directors and actors. Clifford Leech remained General Editor until 1971, and was succeeded by F. David Hoeniger, who retired in 1985.

From 1985 the Revels Plays were under the direction of four General Editors: initially David Bevington, E. A. J. Honigmann, J. R. Mulryne and E. M. Waith. E. A. J. Honigmann retired in 2000 and was succeeded by Richard Dutton. E. M. Waith retired in 2003 and was succeeded by Alison Findlay and Helen Ostovich. Published originally by Methuen, the series is now published by Manchester University Press, embodying essentially the same format, scholarly character and high editorial standards of the series as first conceived. The series concentrates on plays from the period 1558–1642, and includes a small number of non-dramatic works of interest to students of drama. Some slight changes have been made: for example, in editions from 1978 onward, notes to the introduction are placed together at the end, not at the foot of the page. Collation and commentary notes continue, however, to appear on the relevant pages.

The text of each Revels play, in accordance with established practice in the series, is edited afresh from the original text of best authority (in a few instances, texts), but spelling and punctuation are modernised and speech headings are silently made consistent. Elisions in the original are also silently regularised, except where metre would be affected by the change; since 1968 the '-ed' form is used for non-syllabic terminations in past tenses and past participles ('-'d' earlier), and '-èd' for syllabic ('-ed' earlier). The editor emends, as distinct from modernises, the original only in instances where error is patent, or at least very probable, and correction persuasive. Act divisions are given only if they appear in the original or if the structure of the play clearly points to them. Those act and scene divisions not in the original are provided in small type. Square brackets are also used for any other additions to or changes in the stage directions of the original.

Revels Plays do not provide a variorum collation, but only those variants which require the critical attention of serious textual students. All departures of substance from 'copy-text' are listed, including any relineation and those changes in punctuation which involve to any degree a decision between alternative interpretations; but not such accidentals as turned letters, nor necessary additions to stage directions whose editorial nature is already made clear by the use of brackets. Press corrections in the 'copy-text' are likewise collated. Of later emendations of the text, only those are given which as alternative readings still deserve attention.

One of the hallmarks of the Revels Plays is the thoroughness of their annotations. Besides explaining the meaning of difficult words and passages, the editor provides comments on customs or usage, text or stage-business – indeed, on anything judged pertinent and helpful. Each volume contains an Index to the Commentary, in which particular attention is drawn to meanings for words not listed in *OED*, and (starting in 1996) an indexing of proper names and topics in the Introduction and Commentary.

The introduction to a Revels play assesses the authority of the 'copy-text' on which it is based, and discusses the editorial methods employed in dealing with it; the editor also considers the play's date and (where relevant) sources, together with its place in the work of the author and in the theatre of its time. Stage history is offered, and in the case of a play by an author not previously represented in the series a brief biography is given.

It is our hope that plays edited in this fashion will promote further scholarly and theatrical investigation of one of the richest periods in theatrical history.

DAVID BEVINGTON
RICHARD DUTTON
ALISON FINDLAY
J. R. MULRYNE
HELEN OSTOVICH

Acknowledgements

Many scholars and academic institutions have assisted in the preparation of this edition. The British Academy provided me with a travel award, which allowed me to complete the collation of the eight extant copies of the 1597 quarto, and I am grateful both to them and the staff of the British Library, the Bodleian Library, the Victoria and Albert Museum, Worcester College (Oxford), the Houghton Library (Harvard), the Huntington Library, the Lilly Library (University of Indiana, Bloomington), and the Harry Ransom Research Center (University of Texas at Austin) for all the help given to me in the course of the last three years. Among the many friends and colleagues in the United Kingdom who have helped to bring this book to fruition, I would like in particular to record my thanks to Brian Schneider for his suggestions in relation to the commentary, Sue Hall-Smith for her invaluable assistance with the production history of the play, and Robin Griffin for overseeing the translation of all Latin material other than passages quoted from the Loeb editions, numerous points of information on classical topics, and the enthusiastic interest he has brought to the project.

For the photograph of Katharine Hepburn in the role of Pandora that forms the frontispiece to this edition, and my information on the memorable production of *The Woman in the Moon* at Bryn Mawr College in 1928, I have a number of people and institutions to thank. I am grateful to Penguin Books Ltd and Random House Inc. for allowing me to quote Ms Hepburn's own reflections on her role, recorded in her autobiography, *Me* (Alfred A. Knopf, New York, 1991: Penguin Books, 1992), and to Mary Macomber Leue for permitting me to draw on her memories of the occasion. I am indebted to The Academy of Motion Picture Arts and Sciences (Beverly Hills) for supplying the photograph of Ms Hepburn, and to Katharine Houghton for generously allowing me to use it, and supplying me with sources of information on her aunt's attitude to her role. Above all, I would like to thank Kristine Krueger of the Margaret Herrick Library, Motion Picture Academy of Arts and Sciences, for her tireless assistance in the location of photographs of the production, her keen interest in my endeavours, and her help in securing the permissions noted above.

The most signal debt of gratitude I owe, however, in the preparation of this edition is to George K. Hunter and David Bevington, who edited the three volumes of Lyly's plays already published in the Revels series. I cannot hope to emulate their learning, but I have striven to structure my work upon theirs. I count myself extremely fortunate in having had David Bevington's erudite assistance, as General Editor, in the production of this volume.

Abbreviations

ANCIENT TEXTS

Wherever possible, Graeco-Roman texts are cited by the standard reference to book, chapter, and paragraph for prose texts, or to book (where applicable), poem, and line number for verse. All references to Ovid's *Metamorphoses* (*Met.*) are to the translation by Arthur Golding (1567), in the edition by W. H. D. Rouse, published as *Shakespeare's Ovid: being Arthur Golding's translation of the 'Metamorphoses'* (1904, reissued 1961). The Loeb Classical Library (LCL) offers a convenient edition for many classical authors, and all other citations are to the Loeb texts unless otherwise stated.

Cicero	*De officiis.*
Hesiod, *Works and Days*	In *The Homeric Hymns and Homerica.*
Hesiod, *The Theogony*	In *The Homeric Hymns and Homerica.*
Horace, *Carm.*	*Carmena.* In *Odes and Epodes.*
Horace, *Epi.*	*Epistles.*
Hyginus, *Fab.*	*Fabularum liber.* The relevant passage is quoted by Bond, iii, p. 135.
Martial, *Epigr.*	*Epigrammata.*
Ovid, *Am.*	*Amores.*

Ovid, *Ars am.*	*Ars amatoria.*
Ovid, *Her.*	*Heroides.*
Pliny (Gaius Plinius Secundus)	*Natural history.*
Virgil	*Eclogues.*

OTHER ABBREVIATIONS

The place of publication is London unless otherwise indicated. All quotations from the works of Shakespeare are from *The Arden Shakespeare Complete Works*, gen. eds Richard Proudfoot, Ann Thompson and David Scott Kastan (1998, rev., 2001). Abbreviations of the works of Shakespeare are those adopted by the Revels Plays. References to plays other than those by Shakespeare are to the Revels editions.

Alwes   Derek B. Alwes, *Sons and Authors in Elizabethan England* (Newark, 2004).

Anatomy   Euphues: The Anatomy of Wit. See Lyly.

Andreadis   A. Harriette Andreadis, ed., *Mother Bombie*, Elizabethan and Renaissance Studies (Salzburg, 1975).

Barnes   Alexander B. Grosart, ed., *The Poems of Barnabe Barnes* (1875).

Barish   Jonas Barish, 'The Prose Style of John Lyly', *ELH* 23 (1956), 14–35.

Bevington, ed., *Endymion*   See Lyly.

Bible   *The Geneva Bible*, a facsimile of the 1560 edition, intro. Lloyd E. Berry (Madison, Wis., 1969).

Bond   R. Warwick Bond, ed., *The Complete Works of John Lyly*, 3 vols (Oxford, 1902).

Bullough   Geoffrey Bullough, *Narrative and Dramatic Sources of Shakespeare*, 8 vols (1957–75).

Chambers   E. K. Chambers, *The Elizabethan Stage*, 4 vols (Oxford, 1923).

Charney   Maurice Charney, 'Female Roles and the Children's Companies: Lyly's Pandora in *The Woman in the Moon*', *Research Opportunities in Renaissance Drama* XII (1979), 37–43.

Daniel   Carter A. Daniel, ed., *The Plays of John Lyly* (Lewisburg, Pa., 1988).

England   Euphues and His England. See Lyly.

Fairholt   F. W. Fairholt, ed., *The Dramatic Works of John Lilly*, 2 vols (1858).

Greg   W. W. Greg, *A Bibliography of the English Printed Drama to the Restoration*, 4 vols (1939–59).

Hepburn   Katharine Hepburn, *Me: Stories of My Life* (New York, 1991; London, 1992).

Hunter   G. K. Hunter, *John Lyly: The Humanist as Courtier* (1962).

Hunter and Bevington, eds, *Campaspe: Sappho and Phao*   See Lyly.

Hunter and Bevington, eds, *Galatea: Midas*   See Lyly.

Knight   G. Wilson Knight, 'John Lyly', *Review of English Studies* XV (1939), 146–63.

Lancashire   Anne Lancashire, 'John Lyly and Pastoral Entertainment', in G. R. Hibbard, ed., *The Elizabethan Theatre VIII* (Port Meany, 1982), pp. 22–50.

Lyly   References are to the Revels Plays (Manchester) for *Campaspe* and *Sappho and Phao* (ed. George K. Hunter and David Bevington, 1991), *Endymion* (ed. David Bevington, 1996), and *Galatea* and *Midas* (ed.

George K. Hunter and David Bevington, 2000). References to *Euphues: The Anatomy of Wit* and *Euphues and His England* are to the modern-spelling edition in the Revels Plays Companion Library Series (ed. Leah Scragg, Manchester, 2003). All references to *The Woman in the Moon* are to the present edition unless otherwise stated. References to *Pappe with an Hatchet* and plays by Lyly not yet published in the Revels series (i.e. *Love's Metamorphosis* and *Mother Bombie*) are to Bond.

Love's Metamorphosis   See Lyly.

Marston   G. B. Harrison, ed., *The Scourge of Villanie 1599*, Bodley Head Quartos, 13 (1925; reprinted New York, 1974).

The Maydes Metamorphosis   See Bond (who includes the play among Lyly's works).

Milton   Helen Darbishire, ed., *The Poetical Works of John Milton* (1958).

Mother Bombie   See Lyly.

OED   *The Oxford English Dictionary.*

Onions   C. T. Onions, *A Shakespeare Glossary*, enlarged and rev. Robert D. Eagleson (Oxford, 1986).

Pappe   *Pappe with an Hatchet*. See Lyly.

Parthenophil and Parthenope   See Barnes.

Peele   Charles Tyler Prouty, gen. ed., *The Life and Works of George Peele*, 3 vols (New Haven, 1952–70).

Pincombe   Michael Pincombe, *The Plays of John Lyly: Eros and Eliza*, Revels Plays Companion Library Series (Manchester, 1996).

The Rare Triumphs of Love and Fortune   John Isaac Owen, ed., *An Edition of The Rare Triumphs of Love and Fortune* (New York and London, 1997).

Saccio   Peter Saccio, *The Court Comedies of John Lyly: A Study in Allegorical Dramaturgy* (Princeton, NJ, 1969).

Scragg   Leah Scragg, 'The Victim of Fashion? Re-reading the Biography of John Lyly', *Medieval and Renaissance Drama in England* 19 (2006).

Spenser   J. C. Smith and E. de Selincourt, eds, *The Poetical Works of Edmund Spenser* (1912).

STC   A. W. Pollard and G. R. Redgrave, *A Short-Title Catalogue of Books Printed in England, Scotland, and Ireland . . . 1475–1640*, rev. W. A. Jackson, F. S. Ferguson, and K. F. Pantzer, 3 vols (1976–91).

Wilson   Elkin Calhoun Wilson, *England's Eliza* (Cambridge, Mass., 1939).

Introduction

THE TEXT

The Woman in the Moon is first mentioned in a Stationers' Register entry for 1595:

> xxij die Septembris./.
> **Robert Fynche./.** Entred for his Copie vnder thhands of bothe the wardens a booke intitule [*sic*] a woman in the moone   vj^d.[1]

Though Finch was active as a stationer in London between 1595 and 1603, no other work is assigned to him in the Stationers' Register, and there is no evidence that he proceeded to publication. The first extant quarto of *The Woman in the Moon* (STC 17090) did not appear until 1597, when the play was published by William Jones, with no record of a formal transfer of rights. The title-page reads:

> [ornament] / THE WOMAN / in the Moone. / As it was presented before / *her Highnesse.* / By IOHN LYLLIE maister / *of Artes.* / [lace ornament] / *Imprinted at London for William* / Iones, and are to be sold at the signe of the / *Gun, neere Holburne Conduict.* / 1597.

No printer is mentioned on the title-page, but the ornament, a 'frame of arabesque and scroll-work, 122 × 76 mm',[2] links the play with *The Blind Beggar of Alexandria* published by Jones the following year, and the press operated by Gabriel Simson, formerly in partnership with William White,[3] previously employed by Jones on another project.[4]

The text collates A–F4 G2 and has twenty-six unnumbered leaves, the title-page being on A1r and the 'Prologus' (in italics and framed above and below by ornaments) on A1v. Act 1 begins on A2r, below a lace ornament, and a stage direction in large type, but no act or scene heading, and the play concludes, with 'FINIS', on G2r (G2v blank). The text is cleanly printed, with very few typographical errors, but for the assignment of lines 5.1.261 and 283 to *Mer*[*cury*] rather than *Mars* (G1r and G1v), presumably through the similarity of the names in the printer's copy; and a cluster of mistakes, principally of punctuation and capitalization, on D4r, F1v, F2r, and G1v, possibly ascribable, in some instances, to a shortage of type,[5] but

1

sufficiently numerous on F1v and F2r to suggest the work of a less experienced printer.[6] Collation of the eight extant copies of the edition[7] reveals no press variants, but Latin '*Alts*' on C3r (3.1.111) has been corrected, in ink, to '*Alti*' in all extant copies.

The reliability of the text suggests that, like *Campaspe* and *Sappho and Phao* published in 1584, and the cluster of Lyly's court comedies issued by William Brome and his widow subsequent to the closure of Paul's Boys,[8] the play was either prepared by the dramatist himself for publication[9] or was 'very close to what Lyly had written',[10] but it nevertheless differs from these earlier quartos in a number of respects. The names of the characters involved in a scene are listed only when they appear, rather than being grouped at the head of scenes on the classical model, while the ascent and descent of the drama's succession of presiding deities is indicated, with few exceptions, throughout.[11] Costuming and staging are detailed more fully, moreover, than in any previously published Lylian play. The first entrance of the shepherds, for example, is accompanied by the direction '*all clad in Skins*' (A2v: 1.1.30.2), and they leave the stage '*singing a roundelay in praise of* Nature' (A2v: 1.1.54.1). The first appearance of Pandora is effected by means of a precisely delineated spectacle: 'They draw the Curtins from before Natures shop, where stands an Image clad and some vnclad, they bring forth the cloathed image' (A2v: 1.1.56.1–3), and similar detailed directions (often distinguished by a change of font) accompany, among other examples, the bringing of Pandora to life (A3r: 1.1.68–91), the heroine's initial unresponsiveness towards her suitors (A4v–B1r: 1.1.183ff.), and the controversy between the shepherds following the killing of the boar (B4v–C1r: 2.1.181.1ff.). The text is further differentiated from the remainder of the plays published during the dramatist's lifetime, none of which preserves any of the sung material which is a consistent feature of the corpus, by the inclusion of two of the four songs performed in the course of the work (C4r: 3.2.41ff. and F2v: 5.1.8off.), though neither is typographically distinguished in the text.[12] Taken together, these differences imply a greater proximity to the production process than the group of Lylian comedies published by William and Joan Brome, and contribute to the problems of dating, discussed below, that surround the play.

The Woman in the Moon was not republished prior to Lyly's death, and the work was not among the group of comedies registered to Edward Blount in 1628 and subsequently published by him, under the title *Six Court Comedies*, in 1632. The play thus shares with

Love's Metamorphosis the distinction of existing in only one early edition, and it is consequently upon the 1597 quarto that the text of the present edition is based (see 'This edition' below).

DATE AND AUTHORSHIP

The Woman in the Moon is the first play by Lyly to carry his name on the title-page, and his authorship has never been challenged, though the drama differs in a number of ways from the remainder of the corpus.[13] The play is largely written in blank verse, rather than the highly patterned euphuistic prose characteristic of the dramatist's work, with informal prose reserved for a comic servant. The action depends much more heavily upon intricate plotting than any other Lylian play, with the exception of *Mother Bombie*, and operates on multiple levels,[14] rather than through the pattern of symbolic locations integral, in the majority of Lyly's court comedies, to the projection of meaning. Unlike the witty pages or apprentices of *Campaspe, Sappho and Phao, Galatea, Endymion, Midas*, and *Mother Bombie*, whose activities and word-play contribute to the construction of a self-contained dramatic universe, Pandora's servant, Gunophilus, enjoys a collusive relationship with the audience that breaks down the boundary between those inside and outside the play world, giving rise to an actor–audience relationship unique in Lylian drama. Taken together with the textual divergences from the remainder of the canon noted above and the late publication of the work, these differences have led to the conclusion that the play occupies a distinct position in the Lylian corpus, an inference supported by the writer's own comments on the work. The closing lines of the Prologus define the drama as 'a *poet's* dream' (my emphasis), highlighting the departure from the playwright's customary prose form, and the experimental character of the piece is further emphasized by the assertion that the play is 'The first he had in Phoebus' holy bower [i.e. under the aegis of the god of poetry], / But not the last – unless the first displease' (lines 18–19).

The dissimilarity between *The Woman in the Moon* and the rest of Lyly's plays has had a significant bearing on the date conventionally assigned to the work. The use of blank verse, with prose reserved for a comic servant, the intricate plot, multi-level staging, and actor–audience interaction have led, in the words of G. K. Hunter, to the 'natural assumption . . . that Lyly is here writing for the adult actors, forced to this by the inhibition of the boys',[15] while the fact that the promise of further work in a similar vein was apparently not fulfilled has been taken as indicative that the drama was 'not a popular success', and that it was consequently 'the last of Lyly's plays'.[16] The closure of Paul's Boys circa 1590 thus provides for Hunter a terminus a quo for the composition of the play, while the fact that it was registered to Finch in September 1595 affords firm evidence that it was in existence by that date.

The internal evidence upon which the argument for the late positioning of the work is based is supported by the absence from the title-page of the customary announcement that the play was performed by Paul's Boys. Of Lyly's eight dramatic works, all but *The Woman in the Moon* carry some formula to this effect, including *Love's Metamorphosis*, which did not appear until 1601. The play is indebted, moreover, to Greene's *Planetomachia* published in 1585, and is structurally similar to the anonymous *The Rare Triumphs of Love and Fortune* performed at court in 1582 but not published until 1589 (see p. 11 below). In addition, a number of aspects of the drama suggest a close relationship between Lyly's comedy and Shakespeare's *A Midsummer Night's Dream*, giving credence to a date in the early 1590s. As noted above, the Prologus, like Puck in the Shakespearian play, invites the spectators to think of the work in terms of a 'dream' (compare Prologus, line 17 and *MND*, 5.1.423); both comedies resonate with the concept of change; and the man in the moon with his thorn bush figures in some way in both.

For all the wealth of evidence adduced in its support, however, the argument for the positioning of the play subsequent to the demise of Paul's Boys is not as firmly grounded as is generally supposed.[17] The configuration of characters, for example, does not support the contention that the drama was designed for an adult troupe. Like all Lyly's plays with the exception of *Campaspe*, it has a preponderance of female and juvenile roles, and centres, in sharp contrast to contemporary plays for the public stage, not on male but female experience. Of the twenty named parts only four are for adult men (Saturn, Jupiter, Mars, and Sol), the rest of the dramatis personae consisting of women (including the central figure and the presiding deity), inexperienced youths,[18] and boys. Among the last group, two characters, Cupid and Joculus, are described by Pandora as too young to interest her sexually (3.2.52),[19] while a third (Ganymede) is mute, and may have been designed as a trainee role. The play clearly lends itself to performance by children rather than men, and the probability that Lyly was writing with the talents of

the boys for whom his previous plays had been written in mind is
supported by the performance skills demanded by the work. In
common with the rest of Lyly's plays, the action is punctuated by
songs, designed not for a single individual but written in parts
(cf. 3.2.41ff.), while opportunities are provided to exhibit a range of
other musical accomplishments. Pandora complains, for example, of
the 'pipes' and 'fiddling' (1.1.225) accompanying the 'roundelays'
(1.1.222) with which the shepherds seek to rouse her from her
melancholy, while Joculus dances in 3.2 both alone and with
Pandora (lines 37ff.).[20] An occasion is offered for the Latin word-
play that is a consistent feature of Lyly's work for the private stage
(cf. 3.1.101ff.), and classical allusions, designed to appeal to a coterie
audience and exhibit the boys' learning, are deployed by the dramatis personae throughout – regardless of their character or social position (e.g. Gunophilus' quotation from Martial in 5.1: lines 46–7).[21]

It is hard to believe that a writer with Lyly's experience was naive
enough to imagine that a shift from prose to blank verse was suffi-
cient to allow the success of the play in an arena entirely alien from
that for which it was otherwise designed. The closing lines of the
Prologus announce the change of form not as the product of a
professional exigency but as a creative venture (cf. the violation of
expectation announced in the opening lines), aligning the play not
with the fortunes of a particular company but with that process of
experimentation at work in the cluster of Lylian comedies composed
circa 1589. *Midas*, for example, is unique among Lyly's comedies in
that it is overtly designed as a political allegory, while *Mother Bombie*
is indebted to Roman New Comedy, and far more heavily dependent upon the unravelling of a plot than on a 'characteristically'
Lylian patterning of ideas. Given the dramatist's evident openness
to new artistic possibilities,[22] and the prevalence of blank verse by
the late 1580s in plays written for both the court and the public
stage, the use of a new medium in *The Woman in the Moon* may not
be as significant as is generally supposed, but may simply point to
the dramatist's interest in exploring new modes, and in keeping
abreast of literary fashions.

The supporting items of internal evidence adduced by the critical orthodoxy in aid of the proposition that the play was written for
the public stage are also susceptible of challenge. The contention
that the drama exploits the opportunities for multi-level staging
afforded by the public theatres, for example, is heavily influenced
by the monumental old-spelling edition of the play by R. Warwick

Bond, with its panoply of interpolated stage directions. The performance indicators introduced into 3.2 have been particularly influential in terms of the dating of the play, in that Bond refers throughout the scene to a 'trap' and devises stage business in relation to its use (e.g. '*Pointing to a trapdoor*', 'STESIAS *descends through the trap*', '*The trap rises slightly*').[23] Though the play, as noted above, is unusually rich in stage directions, no mention is made of a trapdoor – the place of hiding to which the term is assigned by Bond being described in both text and stage directions as a 'cave' (compare 3.2.192, 221, 228, 252, 325.1). The 'cave' is a familiar 'house' or stage property in Tudor drama,[24] and is used by Lyly himself in *Sappho and Phao*, a play produced at both the court and the Blackfriars, and thus capable of performance in a private theatre venue. More significantly, the cave is one of the two principal locations of the action of *The Rare Triumphs of Love and Fortune*, a work to which *The Woman in the Moon* is indebted in a range of other respects, and which is the subject of an entry for 1582–83 in the Revels accounts. The entry records that 'newe provision was made of one Citty and one Battlement of Canvas iij Ells of sarcenet A [blank] of canvas, and viij. paire of gloves with sundrey other furniture'.[25] Though the structure for which the canvas was supplied is unfortunately unspecified, it is generally taken to be the cave before which much of the action takes place and to which the characters travel from the 'Citty'.[26] The entry points to the probability that Lyly's cave, which may well look back to that of the earlier play, was a comparable structure,[27] and this probability is heightened by other similarities in the staging of the two works. In both, the action is overseen by presiding deities, effected in *Love and Fortune* by the use of a canvas 'Battlement', defined by Chambers as 'any platform provided for action at a higher level than the floor of the stage'.[28] The fact that Lyly's planets 'enter' and then 'ascend' rather than appearing 'above' suggests that their dominance was similarly effected by means of an on-stage structure, and was thus not dependent upon the availability of an upper stage.

The play's suitability for a performance space lacking the facilities of the public theatres is confirmed by the title-page of the 1597 quarto. In common with the majority of Lyly's comedies, the play 'was presented before her Highnesse', and it may consequently be expected to operate within the staging limitations of drama written for the court. Significantly, these limitations do not exclude the use of polarized locations, either horizontally, as in Lyly's *Campaspe*, with the opposition between the 'houses' of Apelles and Diogenes, or vertically, as in *The Rare Triumphs of Love and Fortune*, where the horizontal balance between cave and city intersects with a vertical contrast between the abode of the gods on the 'battlement' and that of the fiends who rise through a trapdoor. While the use of the trap in the anonymous play complicates the argument about the nature of Lyly's cave,[29] it serves to confirm that multi-level staging is not exclusive to work produced for the public stage. Similarly, Peele's *The Arraignment of Paris* (c.1584), which also involves the use of a trapdoor,[30] supplies incontrovertible evidence that multi-level staging has no bearing on the nature of the company, as opposed to the venue, for which a particular play was designed. Not only was Peele's play presented before the Queen, it was performed not by men like the anonymous play, but by the Children of the Chapel.

The use of an intricate plot and interaction between those inside and outside the play world are equally unreliable witnesses to the provenance of the work, in that neither is exclusive to material written for the public stage. *Mother Bombie*, the most intricately plotted of Lyly's plays, was performed by Paul's Boys, while the 'Shakespearian' relationship between Gunophilus and the audience is frequently found in Tudor drama (e.g. in Medwall's *Fulgens and Lucrece*)[31] and may well derive in this instance from the actor/audience relationships of *The Rare Triumphs of Love and Fortune*. Not only does the comic servant Lentulo, in the related play, interact with those outside the play world (e.g. at lines 641ff.), but so does the parasite Penulo (lines 1194ff.), the disaffected Vulcan (lines 251-2), and even the hero, Hermione (lines 1370-1).[32] Shakespeare's indebtedness to Lyly in a range of plays composed in the 1590s is well attested, and the similarities between *The Woman in the Moon* and Shakespearian drama in this (and other) respects does not distinguish the work in terms of either date or provenance from other items (e.g. *Galatea*, *Endymion*) in the Lylian corpus.

The textual evidence afforded by the differences between the 1597 quarto and the plays published by William and Joan Brome is also less significant than it appears at first sight. The movement away from the mass grouping of characters at the head of a scene on the classical model towards the modern practice of indicating when characters enter and leave the stage is not found solely in *The Woman in the Moon* but forges a further link with *Mother Bombie*, another play which stands aside, in terms of late publication, from the majority of Lyly's plays. The development may be indicative that the dramatist was less involved in the publication of these works than in that of the more self-consciously literary quartos,[33] but can have no bearing on the nature of the company for which *The Woman in the Moon* was designed, in that *Mother Bombie* was written for a juvenile troupe. Similarly, the detailed indication of stage business is not a fresh departure in Lyly's work, but may be seen in terms of a progression. As Hunter notes, 'as a representation of the theatrical event' the quarto of *Galatea* must 'be distinguished from its predecessors, *Campaspe* and *Sappho and Phao*', in that whereas those plays are 'represented in print within the strict limits appropriate to the presentation of classical dramatic texts', in *Galatea* 'we are given a fuller picture of stage business', with 'mid-scene entries marked [and] some (minimal) stage directions'.[34] The same distinction is evident between these early quartos and that of *Endymion* (1591), shown, for example, in the detailed description of the dumb show following 3.2.67, and of the action following the entrance of the fairies (4.3.32.1–2). The fact that the quarto of *Midas* (1592) reverts to the practice of the two earliest plays, with no indication of 'needed props' or 'theatrical effects',[35] is indicative of the difficulty of constructing a chronology of the work on the basis of evidence that may have more bearing on the author's degree of involvement in the preparation of his plays for publication than on the order in which they were written.

The questionable nature of the evidence that the play was written for the adult stage admits the possibility that the work was not composed after the inhibition of Paul's Boys but antedates the company's closure. As noted above, a number of features of the work exhibit its proximity to *Mother Bombie*, and a complex of other influences and echoes strengthen the case for composition circa 1590. The play looks back to Greene's *Planetomachia* (1585) and belongs to the same 'highly specialized'[36] dramatic genre as *The Rare Triumphs of Love and Fortune*, performed, as noted above, in 1582 but not published until 1589. Lyly's own *Pappe with an Hatchet*, also published in 1589 and reissued the same year, is echoed (or anticipated) on a number of occasions,[37] while the dramatist's failure to fulfil his promise to produce more plays in a similar vein may be a product not of the play's failure but of the closure of the company in which he was deeply embedded and for which he habitually wrote.

The possibility that *The Woman in the Moon* was written prior to the closure of Paul's Boys has important ramifications for the construction of Lyly's career. Whereas the silence of his later years is generally attributed to his failure to adapt to changing artistic demands, the inventiveness displayed in *Midas, Mother Bombie,* and *The Woman in the Moon* does not support the proposition that their author was too wedded to a particular style of coterie drama to respond to rapidly evolving theatrical tastes and conditions. Though a reconsideration of his career and reputation lies outside the scope of this introduction,[38] the possibility that *The Woman in the Moon* may have been composed circa 1590 must cast doubt on some of the assumptions regarding his biography underpinning contemporary Lylian studies.

SOURCES

The story of the creation of Pandora and her destructive influence on mankind is first related by Hesiod (*Works and Days*, lines 69ff. and *Theogony*, lines 570–612). Hesiod describes how Zeus, angered by the theft of fire from heaven by Prometheus, instructed Hephestion to create the first woman, and ordered the gods to endow her with their qualities. He then bestowed this new creation, Pandora (i.e. all-gifted), on Epimetheus, brother of the offending mortal, who accepted it, forgetting Prometheus' warning of the danger of accepting gifts from the gods. Pandora subsequently opened the lid of a jar containing every human ill, and released its contents into the world, hope alone remaining at the bottom of the vessel to be a comfort to afflicted humankind. The story, briefly retold in Hyginus' *Fabularum liber* (Fab. 142),[39] offers a misogynistic account of the origins of the evils and sufferings of human life, and was well known in the Renaissance, but the version of the myth presented by Lyly differs from the inherited narrative in a number of respects. The supreme deity in the Lylian drama is not a malign Zeus, with Hephestion as his instrument, but a benign Nature, while the gifts bestowed on Pandora at her creation are uniformly positive, though they are later perverted by the negative influence of the planets. No reference is made in the play to the jar with its cargo of suffering, though Pandora does bring distress to her husband and lovers, and no mention is made of any residual hope to mitigate the male protagonists' hardship and loss.

A number of Lyly's changes to the myth may derive, as Bond noted,[40] from Geoffrey Fenton's *Certaine Tragicall Discourses* (1567, 2nd ed. 1579), a work consisting of a selection of stories translated from Belleforest's *Histoires Tragiques*.[41] Fenton's third tale concerns Pandora, 'a yong lady in Mylan', created, according to her lover Parthonope, by 'The curious Artificer and coninge worke woman Dame Nature', who 'was not so careful to worke [her] in her semelie frame of all perfections, as the powers deuine and disposers of the daungerous and loftye planets, (assistinge her endeuour with certaine peculier ornaments of their speciall grace) weare redye to open their golden vessell of precious treasur powring by great abundance their heauenly gifts vpon [her]'. For all her initial endowments, however, Pandora's life from her earliest years 'gaue manyfest signes' that her disposition was adversely affected by a 'poysined Clymatte which firste gettynge domynion ouer the yonge yeares of her grene vnderstanding dyrected after yᵉ whole seaquel of her life by the dyal of a cursed constellacion'. The implied tension here between a beneficent Nature, assisted by 'powers deuine', and the 'daungerous and loftye planets' lies at the heart of Lyly's play, and the gamut of vices Fenton's Pandora exhibits lends weight to the argument that the drama and the prose work are related. Just as Lyly's heroine is subject to planetary influence causing her to be, in turn, sullen, proud, aggressive, amiable, amorous, treacherous, and fickle, so Fenton's Pandora was 'disdaynfull without respect, spytefull without measure, honge altogether full of the fethers of folyshe pryde [and] so whollye gyuen to wallowe in dilycacie that she detested al exercises of vertue'.[42]

Whereas in Fenton's work the influence of the planets on human life is incidental and merely implied, it is integral to Greene's *Planetomachia* (1585),[43] to which *The Woman in the Moon* may also look back. Greene's narrative is structured upon a contest between Venus (supported by Mars and Mercury) and Saturn (supported by Jupiter and Luna), each of whom accuses the other of a prejudicial effect on earthly affairs. Each of the disputants recounts a story exhibiting the malign influence of the other, while Sol is appointed to arbitrate over their competing claims. His judgement precipitates a further quarrel, this time between Jupiter and Mars, leading to a third story, recounted by Jupiter, demonstrating the dangers of an addiction to war.[44] The first two stories, of Rodento and Pasylla (presented by Venus) and Rhodope and Psamnetichus (presented by Saturn), are ruthlessly plagiarized from *Euphues: The Anatomy of Wit* (Venus' tale) and *Euphues and His England* (Saturn's tale), the originality of the work lying exclusively in the dialogue form employed, and the astronomical framework within which the narratives are set.

The quarrel between the planets is dramatic in its effect, while the destructive influence of the constellations is evident throughout. In a pleasing instance of intertextual circularity, it is these aspects of Greene's work which may have fed into Lyly's play,[45] though the case for direct indebtedness is complicated by the similarities between both compositions and an anonymous play, *The Rare Triumphs of Love and Fortune*, performed at court by Derby's men in 1582 but not published until 1589.

Though *The Rare Triumphs of Love and Fortune* makes no mention of the myth of Pandora, it anticipates *The Woman in the Moon*, as noted above, in a number of respects. Once again, the work is predicated upon a quarrel between deities, in this instance Venus and Fortune, each of whom claims supremacy over human affairs, and whose dispute is the subject of divine arbitration, in this case by Jupiter in the presence of an assembly of the gods. As in Greene's *Planetomachia*, the contest is conducted by means of an exemplary tale, but in the drama the story is enacted rather than related, and directly influenced by the competing deities who, as in Lyly's play, direct and oversee the action throughout. At the close of the first act, Jupiter explicitly announces that a human couple are to serve as the testing ground of the competing deities' powers (lines 257–66), and instructs the goddesses to 'take vp your places heere to woorke your will' (line 271). The direction implies that Venus and Fortune remain on stage, and their positioning above the level of the human action is indicated by Vulcan's comment that 'They are set a sunning like a Crow in a gutter' (line 273). In Act 5, in a scene comparable with that in which Lyly's Jupiter, also positioned aloft, elects to 'discuss' the 'heavenly cloud' that hides him from view and disclose himself to Pandora (*The Woman in the Moon*, 2.1.21ff.), Venus declares that 'Hye time it is that now we did appeare' (line 1741), an announcement prefaced by the stage direction, '*Venus and Fortune shew themselues and speak to Phizantius, while Hermione standeth in a maze*'. The emphasis on the manipulation of human affairs by supernatural powers, and the use of multi-level staging as a visual metaphor for this relationship, forges a significant link between the two plays, and the likelihood that Lyly was indebted to the earlier drama is strengthened by the use of a 'cave' as a place of concealment (see p. 6 above), and the collusive interplay, in both compositions, between comic characters and those outside the play world – a device limited in Lyly's earlier plays to the more formal addresses of prologues and epilogues (see p. 7 above).[46]

While the fusion of a network of narratives exhibiting the intervention of the gods in the human sphere supplies one strand of the
interwoven complex of sources from which *The Woman in the Moon*
is constructed, a second thread is supplied by the fable of the man
in the moon. The geographical features visible on the surface of the
moon have long been associated with the figure of a man, bearing
a thorn bush on his back, and accompanied, in some traditions, by
a dog (cf. *A Midsummer Night's Dream*, 5.1.251–3), and a number of
folk tales, often turning upon some act of transgression, account for
his appearance. In one of the 'Harley Lyrics', for example, written
in the late thirteenth (or early fourteenth) century, the figure is that
of a rustic thief, his clothes torn by thorns, caught in the act of
stealing a bundle of sticks from a hedge,[47] and it is this story which
appears to lie behind Henryson's reference in 'The Testament of
Cresseid' to the man in the moon as a thief, prevented by his offence
from ascending any closer to heaven (lines 260–3).[48] The notion of
wrongdoing links these accounts with fables identifying the figure
with the man stoned to death for gathering wood on the Sabbath
(Numbers, xv.32–6), or Cain, bearing the bundle of sticks for the
sacrifice unacceptable to God (Genesis, iv.3–5).[49] The placing of the
man in the moon as a punishment finds an echo in Lyly's drama,
in that it is an offence against the commands of Nature that results
in the banishment of both Gunophilus and Stesias to Luna's sphere
at the close of the play. In Lyly's version of the narrative, however,
the former is not merely placed in the moon as a punishment for
his revolt against Nature's commands. He is transformed into a
thorn bush, which Stesias, in a fit of anger at his own fate, elects to
carry on his back, master and man thus combining to supply the
characteristic features of the man in the moon.

It is not the origin of the thorn bush, however, that constitutes
Lyly's most radical departure from the complex of folk tales on
which he draws. The Prologus announces that the story of the play
ranges 'A point beyond the ancient theoric' (line 3), in that the
dramatist 'Hath seen a woman [rather than the conventional man]
seated in the moon' (line 2).[50] Lyly's play thus offers an alternative
version of the inherited story, paralleling his 'revisionist'[51] treatment
of the myth in an earlier play, *Endymion*, performed before the
Queen in 1588.[52] Like *The Woman in the Moon*, *Endymion* brings
together a classical story (in this instance that of the love of
the Moon for the mortal Endymion), and the folk tale regarding the
figure visible on the moon's surface, reversing in both cases the

terms of the traditional narrative, in that in this version of the story it is not the deity who is in love with the mortal, but the mortal who is enamoured of the deity, while the man in the moon is not a wrong-doer but a faithful lover attendant on his mistress. The sub-title of the earlier play, *The Man in the Moon*, suggests that *The Woman in the Moon* may have been designed, in part, as a companion piece, and the outcome of the later play may be seen in terms of a misogynistic reversal of the closing scenes of the earlier work. Not only is the ever-changing Pandora established as the 'unmovable' (*Endymion*, 1.1.36) Cynthia's substitute, ruling the moon in her place, but she is followed not by a faithful lover content to spend his life in 'sweet contemplation' of his mistress (*Endymion*, 5.4.173) but by a disillusioned, antagonistic husband, longing for an oppor-tunity to scratch her face with the thorn bush he bears for ever on his back (*The Woman in the Moon*, 5.1.324–5).

While the use of the name Pandora draws attention to one strand of the dramatist's source material, and the play's title to another, inviting audience recognition from the outset of the reversals at work in the course of the play, a third familiar narrative underlying the action is not overtly announced but merely implied. The creation of Pandora at the start of the play runs directly counter to the biblical version of the nature and origins of the human race, challenging the accepted relationships between female and male. Whereas in the Bible humankind is created by a male God, who first gives life to man in his own image, and then to woman, man's inferior, from the body of man himself (Genesis, i.27 and ii.21–3), in *The Woman in the Moon* the prime creator is female, while her most perfect crea-tion, 'the glory of [her] words and work' (1.1.119), is woman rather than man. The play opens with the entrance of Nature, with her two female attendants, and it is Nature, with the help of her assistants, who creates Pandora, not from man but the elements in their purest form, and endows her with 'life and soul' (1.1.67). The terms in which the creation of the first woman is described resonate with biblical echoes, and the possibility that the play will turn on a fall from an Edenic state is implied by the announcement, when she is endowed with the gift of speech, that 'from that root will many mis-chiefs grow / If once she spot her state of innocence' (1.1.85–6). Her first exchange with Nature, with its references to her 'understand-ing soul', her recognition of 'the difference twixt good and bad' (1.1.89–90), and role as 'a solace unto men' (1.1.91), would all have served to establish her, for a sixteenth-century Christian spectator,

as a type or version of Eve, and the initial assumptions of the planets
confirm this construction, while serving to emphasize the distance
between Lyly's heroine and her biblical antecedent. Saturn alludes
to her as a 'new-found gaud' (1.1.109), unconsciously calling attention to the alternative universe evoked in the play through his con-
temptuous description of her as 'A second man, less perfect than
the first' (1.1.110). The comment implies that her position in the
order of nature corresponds to that of the biblical account, and runs
directly counter to that of the presiding deity, who promises the
Utopian shepherds that she will be 'Like to yourselves, but of a purer
mould' (1.1.52).

The inversion of the biblical narrative, like the adaptations to
Hesiod's story of the origins of human suffering and the variations
woven on the myth of the man in the moon, contributes to the
creation of a gynocentric universe, locating the drama, on one level,
within the context of Elizabethan court panegyric. Nature reigns
supreme in the world of the play and both male and female planets
are obliged to defer to her will – a situation patently analogous with
that of the arena in which the work was performed. At the same
time, however, the implications of the title of the drama challenge
the play's application to contemporary reality. The proverbial phrase
'the man in the moon' denoted, in the sixteenth century, the unat-
tainable or ludicrously far-fetched, and was employed to suggest
scepticism or outright disbelief. The title of the play thus serves to
invite incredulity from the outset, at once tactfully distancing its
author from serious intent (cf. the more explicit disclaimer of the
Prologue to *Endymion*),[53] while questioning the credibility of the
universe he exhibits.

The fusion of classical, folk tale, biblical, and proverbial material
into an elegant structure that interrogates, through the exhibition of
alternative potentialities, the concepts embedded in the inherited
stories and the assumptions of sixteenth-century culture is characteristic of Lyly's work. The two parts of *Euphues*, for example, draw
(among a vast range of sources) on the biblical tale of the prodigal
son, the love-and-friendship tradition, the works of Ovid, Caesar,
and Plutarch, and folk-lore charms for inducing love, while
Endymion, an eclectic combination 'of classical and native traditions',[54] marries the myth of Endymion with the *miles gloriosus* of
classical drama, the love-and-friendship tradition, the magical fountain of medieval romance, and the fairies of European folk tale. The
breadth of reference serves to create a universe divorced, in both

plays and prose works, from any specific temporal space, and the arena of the action is further expanded by the host of incidental literary allusions that permeate the texts. In *The Woman in the Moon* numerous classical myths are woven into the texture of the play (e.g. of Danae, Leda, Callisto, Europa, Ariadne, Daphne, Thetis, Tantalus),[55] while a range of classical authors is echoed or directly quoted in the course of the work. Ovid's *Metamorphoses*, for example, underlies Nature's opening description of the universe she governs (1.1.5–12), and the same work is alluded to at 3.2.185–9 and 5.1.286. Other Ovidian material is quoted at 3.2.54 (*Ars amatoria*), 4.1.28 (*Amores*) and 4.1.138–9 (*Heroides*), while Horace's *Epistles*, Cicero's *De officiis*, and Martial's *Epigrammata* are drawn on at 3.2.17, 5.1.123–4, and 5.1.46–7. The attributes of the deities bestowed upon Pandora by Nature derive from the Homeric epithets applied to the gods (1.1.103–4), contrasting, in the epic grandeur of the universe they suggest, with the sylvan world of the satyrs evoked by Joculus in 3.2, and the pastoral plains and meadows of the Utopian shepherds.

While evoking a complex reality situated at the start of human history and informed with Greek, Roman, and medieval learning, the sources brought together in *The Woman in the Moon* document the eclecticism of late sixteenth-century culture. Born into a family of humanist scholars and educated at Oxford University, Lyly is typical in terms of his reading of an educated man of his age. In a paradox typical of the author, the play thus affirms its distance from contemporary reality (a Utopian 'nowhere') while affording the twenty-first-century reader an accurate reflection of the mental landscape of the Elizabethan cultural elite.

STRUCTURE

As in a host of other respects, *The Woman in the Moon* differs in terms of its structure from the rest of the Lylian canon. Whereas the majority of Lyly's plays are noted for the intricacy of their design, with groups of characters moving towards and away from one another in a 'dance-like progression'[56] that allows for the exploration of a variety of debate topics through an assemblage of contrasting positions,[57] *The Woman in the Moon* is superficially less complex in organization, appearing to revert to a style of dramaturgy already outdated when the play was composed. The separation of the play world into two distinct spheres, with supernatural beings situated

aloft to exhibit their dominance over the action; the division of the
material into five acts, largely coinciding with the ascendancy of a
particular planet; and the sequential enactment of the temperaments
induced by the influence of the presiding deities, all point to an
emblematic representation of experience in terms of a series of
'shows', at one with the procedures of early Tudor drama (and of
the source play, *The Rare Triumphs of Love and Fortune*), but remote
from the sophistication of the dramatist's previous compositions.

The structure of *The Woman in the Moon* is much less straightforward, however, than it appears at first sight. Across the series of
superficially self-contained segments in which the influence of the
successive planets is exhibited, Lyly develops an evolving intrigue
action that reaches Jonsonian heights of complexity by the fourth
act of the play. The motive for the planets' hostility to Pandora,
leading to the formulation of their plan to defeat Nature's purposes,
is clearly established in Act 1, and the initial success of their strategy to subject the central figure to their influence is evident by the
close of the first scene. The order in which the planets subsequently
dominate the action, however, while initially determined on a hier-
archical basis (see 1.1.132ff.), is then used by the dramatist to
promote an increasingly intricate plot. Thus the arrogance induced
by Jupiter, who succeeds Saturn at the start of Act 2, together with
the former's susceptibility to Pandora's beauty, arouses the wrath of
Juno, who instructs Mars to take Jupiter's place, precipitating the
violence that leads to the wounding of Stesias. Pandora's regret
under the influence of Sol at the wounds she has inflicted results in
her marriage to the man she has injured and the consequent rejection of her other suitors. Her entry into the amatory sphere then
develops with the ascension of Venus into unselective lust, fuelled
by the desires of the unmarried shepherds, now deprived of any hope
of a mate, drawing all the dramatis personae into a welter of deceit
under Mercury's influence in Act 4. By this stage in the play, the
action has moved a considerable distance from the stylized sequential formula to which it appears, initially, to adhere. The expansion
of the planets' influence, through Pandora's conduct, from the
heroine herself to those around her, creates a radically unstable
world that reaches a climax of frenetic activity and conflicting purposes as Pandora seeks to protect her position and revenge herself
upon those who have betrayed her, while her husband and lovers
pursue vengeance for the deceptions practised upon them. The
ascendancy of Luna at the start of Act 5, signalling a world governed

by flux, thus coincides with the physical and mental states already obtaining in the human sphere, while the madness her dominance induces in Pandora may be seen as a product of the heroine's conflicting experiences in the course of the play. Pandora's decision, at the close of Act 5, to occupy the moon as a place best suited to her disposition, thus emerges as the logical outcome of preceding events, completing the shifting emphasis at work in the drama from divine instigation to human agency. The interplay between the inherited, stylized structure and the evolving intrigue plot thus affords two contrasting perspectives (divinely ordained / character-driven) upon the universe the characters inhabit, giving rise to that 'doubleness'[58] characteristic of Lyly's work.

The increasing complexity of the play's action from an initial exposition, through a process of gathering momentum, to a seemingly insoluble network of cross-purposes, finally resolved through the establishment of a new order in conformity with the desires of the central figure, has obvious analogies with the procedures of Roman New Comedy, and other features of the drama invite its location within the Terentian formula.[59] The action opens with a 'Prologus', rather than the customary 'Prologue' (cf. *Campaspe*, *Sappho and Phao*, etc.), and is divided into five acts, all set in Utopia and largely in a single location.[60] The action is single, in that it is solely concerned with the planets' revenge for Pandora's creation, and there are increasingly pointed indications that the dramatist is observing the unity of time.[61] The later acts of the play, which occupy the latter half of a single day, are clearly continuous, and, though no overt reference is made to the morning in the course of the early scenes, the fact that the action takes place in the first half of the day may be inferred from the timing of the banquet in Act 3. Following Gunophilus' completion of an errand arising from events at the close of 2.1, Pandora decides to feast the shepherds in the course of 3.2, and entertains them in the same scene, her departure to meet Learchus, when a quarrel breaks out among her guests suggesting that the banquet is held in the middle of the day. The inference is confirmed by a comment in the following act which establishes that evening has not yet come (4.1.105), and by a series of increasingly pointed references, throughout the concluding scenes, which chart the progress of the late afternoon, early evening and night. At 4.1.207 Pandora sends Melos away with the promise to see him again 'as the sun goes down', while she agrees to meet Learchus 'in the evening' (4.1.230) and Iphicles at 'midnight'

(4.1.170). At 4.1.252 it is clear that the encounter between Melos and Iphicles takes place while it is still daylight, as the former is engaged in wishing for the sun to set, while the fact that time has moved on by the close of the act is indicated by Learchus' announcement that 'evening's past, yea midnight is at hand' (4.1.305). The ascension of Luna at the start of the last act confirms the night-time setting of the final scene, and the implication that the action concludes during the hours of darkness is further promoted by Pandora's decision to take Cynthia's place in the moon.

The order in which the planets dominate the action also contributes to the underlying implication that the action conforms to the pattern of the day. Pandora is described at her creation as 'a second sun' (1.1.80) and her emergence into life from the elements may be seen as a species of dawn. The darkness of mind associated with Saturn, the first of the planets to govern the action, is succeeded by the confidence and strength of Jupiter and Mars, giving way to the ascendancy of Sol at the noon-time centre of the play. The second half of the drama begins with the heat associated with Venus, followed by the shadowy world of Mercury, and ultimately the moonlit environment of Luna and the Woman in the Moon herself. At the same time, however, the scale of the action implied by the intervention of the deities contributes to a very different time scheme at work in the world of the play. While on one level the action conforms to the rhythms of Roman New Comedy, on another it expands into a much larger temporal space, affording the concerns of the play a mythic significance. At the outset of the action, for example, the endowing of Pandora with life is located in a creative continuum by the presence of other, still-lifeless figures awaiting their future role in Nature's shop, while the existence of the shepherds is supplied with a starting point outside the immediate focus of the action by the planets' derisive reference to their creation (1.1.109–10). Allusions by Jupiter and Sol to their previous amours (2.1.13–18 and 3.2.5–11) locate their admiration of Pandora in the context of a recurrent cycle of encounters between deities and mortals, while reported actions within the drama violate its implied narrowness of scope. Pandora comments, for example, when under the influence of Jupiter, that 'By day I think of nothing but of rule; / By night my dreams are all of empery' (2.1.8–9), suggesting that Jove's ascendancy lasts for substantially longer than the Terentian structure implies, and Pandora's relationship with her shepherd lovers invites the same inference in relation to the dominance of

Venus. Learchus recalls, for example the 'thousand kisses' she bestowed on him (4.1.21); Melos remembers 'How oft [he] leant on her silver breast' (4.1.23), and the amorous encounters that took place between them 'ere [he] slept' (4.1.27); while Iphicles recalls the 'sweet pastime' (4.1.25) he enjoyed with her when awake. The comments encourage the audience to imagine a protracted period of sexual intimacy between the heroine and the three men, and Stesias' evolution in the course of the play from a young lover to a jealous husband sustains the illusion that the time span of the action is considerably longer than a single day.

The double time scheme of the drama contributes to that evasiveness which is a distinguishing feature of Lyly's work. Pandora's association with the moon invites an awareness of both narrow (nocturnal/diurnal), and more expansive (lunar) temporal cycles, and the action of the play may be located within both. At the same time, however, the promise made to the deities at the close of the play that each of them will 'glance at [Pandora] in [their] aspects, / And in conjunction dwell with her a space' (5.1.335-6) removes the action from any mundane temporal limitations, endowing it – by supplying an explanation for the progress of the planets – with the timelessness appropriate to a drama engaged in the construction of a species of myth.

MYTH AND METAMORPHOSIS

Unlike a number of the dramatist's previous compositions, *The Woman in the Moon* makes no direct avowal of its evasiveness or resistance to final analysis. Where the Epilogue to *Sappho and Phao* defines the preceding action in terms of a 'labyrinth of conceits' (line 3), and the Prologue to *Endymion* asserts, in an allusion to the subtitle of the work, that 'there liveth none under the sun that knows what to make of the Man in the Moon' (lines 8–9), Lyly's last comedy overtly conforms to the pattern of a 'just-so' story, offering a straightforward, and highly misogynistic, account of the origins of the female disposition. From the moment of her creation, Pandora, the first woman, runs, under the influence of a succession of planets, through a gamut of shifting moods, creating disharmony through her sullenness, pride, and aggression; promoting sexual licence, trickery, and theft; and finally electing to remain eternally 'idle, mutable, / Forgetful, foolish, fickle, frantic, [and] mad' (5.1.313–14) because those 'be the humours that content [her] best' (5.1.315).

Her essential fickleness of being is confirmed by her decision to identify herself with Luna at the close of the play, while Nature's endorsement of that choice, and concluding pronouncement that Pandora-as-Cynthia will henceforward preside over 'women's nuptials, and their birth' (5.1.328), promotes an interpretation of the action as an 'etiological fable',[62] simultaneously anatomizing the female temperament and supplying an explanation for its inherent instability.

The disposition embodied in Pandora and defined in Nature's penultimate speech ('mutable . . . / Fantastical . . . foolish . . . / And stark mad when they cannot have their will': 5.1.329–32) accords with both sixteenth-century constructions of the nature of women[63] and the misogynistic tenor of the myth regarding the origins of the woes of the human race first recorded in Hesiod's *Works and Days* (see p. 9 above). Though no mention is made in the play of Pandora's box, containing all the evils suffered by humankind, Lyly's heroine 'is herself her box'[64] in that it is her unstable personality that brings strife and sorrow to the world of the play. The harmony between Nature and her creations, man and wife, servant and master, neighbour and neighbour, is progressively violated through her influence as the action evolves, and the closing lines, with their resentment and threat of violent retribution (cf. 5.1.319, 322–5, and 337–8), project a condition of strife and dissatisfaction, directly attributable to her creation, into the infinite future beyond the scope of the drama. The action thus conforms to the social attitudes in force beyond the world of the play, implicitly endorsing contemporary constructions of the destructive waywardness of the female mind.

For all its seeming lack of complication, however, *The Woman in the Moon* admits a reading wholly at odds with the misogynism of both sixteenth-century gender discourse and the myth that the name Pandora evokes, affirming its affinity with the rest of the Lylian canon through its capacity to yield 'divers significations'.[65] As noted above, the creation of the first woman enacted in the opening scene is markedly at odds with the biblical account on which the physical and mental inferiority of women is predicated in western European Christian society (see pp. 13–14). Far from being a secondary creation, Lyly's Pandora is Nature's prime achievement, formed from the purest elements (1.1.62), unique (1.1.64), 'matchless' (1.1.63), and of a 'purer mould' (1.1.52) than man, and the admiration that she engenders among gods and mortals confirms her position as the cynosure of the play world. Her rationality and understanding of morality is confirmed in her opening lines (1.1.87–90), and her innocent condition prior to the intervention of the planets is affirmed by Nature herself (1.1.86). Her departure from her prelapsarian state is not, moreover, the product, as in the Christian tradition, of a conscious choice on her own part. It is the malice of the offended gods that whirls her from one cast of mind to the next, and her ultimate lack of responsibility for her behaviour is confirmed in the final scene. Whereas at the outset of the play Nature informs her that if she uses her gifts well she will be her friend and that if she misuses them she will become her foe (1.1.105–6), she salutes the heroine at the close as 'my Pandora' (5.1.292), implicitly exonerating her of misconduct, while the planets who have manipulated her are rebuked as 'envious' (5.1.273), and her deceived husband and servant are punished. The continuance of Nature's favour is indicated, moreover, by the liberty that she affords Pandora, in the last scene, to choose her own temperament and sphere, and by the dominion with which finally she endows her over all future members of her sex.

The positive representation of the heroine, and the stance of the presiding deity towards her, give rise to a much more complex account of the female predicament than the play's adherence to literary and social traditions appears at first sight to allow. Rather than simply rehearsing the stereotypical, negative view of woman as the irrational agent of earthly discord, the play presents her much more sympathetically, as an essentially innocent victim or puppet, manipulated by forces beyond her control. Lyly's Pandora becomes fickle, unstable, and ultimately lunatic not because of her inherent depravity or susceptibility to temptation, but because of the influence of authority figures, who dictate the behaviour she exhibits. Not only do the predominantly male planets construct her, in turn, in their own image, and oblige her to play a variety of roles – subsequently regretting, in some instances, the very dispositions they themselves have induced (cf. 2.1.77–8) – but the shepherds, at whose suit she is created, assail her with conflicting demands, and then castigate her for both meeting and disappointing their wishes. Having agreed to marry Stesias, for example, she is wooed by Learchus, Melos, and Iphicles, each of whom is eager for her to be unfaithful to her husband and willing to betray his own friends, but ready to condemn her for infidelity and sexual licence on the discovery of her relationships with others (cf. 4.1.12ff.), and then to revenge themselves on her for actions they have promoted. Her unstable disposition is thus presented not as innate but induced, the product of conditions beyond her control, while her final decision to embrace her instability is not an act of self-recognition but a means of empowerment, affording her both a coherent identity and a means of negotiating the conflicting demands of her world. The play may thus be seen as a just-so story with a very different purport from that outlined above, exhibiting not how the female character *became* shifting and unstable, but how it was *made* shifting and unstable by the competing imperatives and confused values of a predominantly patriarchal society.[66]

The destiny embraced by Pandora at the close of the play, however, locates her progress in a considerably larger mythical context than that of an etiological fable of either female delinquency or subjection. The attributes she finally embodies, conventionally regarded as negative, and deplored by her husband and the Utopian shepherds, are not repudiated by the dramatist, but aligned with the structure of the universe and the creative process itself. Nature enters at the start of the play accompanied by two seemingly incompatible attendants – Concord and Discord – and the joint role of her handmaids in the promotion of her work is stressed in the opening lines. Though Discord repines at Concord's unification of her heterogeneous creations, Nature insists that in her service, their opposing tendencies must 'prove but one' in that 'Nature works her will from contraries' (1.1.26 and 29). The conflicting principles combine in the 'holy work' (1.1.55) of the creation of Pandora, and it is through their agency that 'new wonders' (1.1.56) are brought into the world.

The concept of a universe founded upon the unification of antithetical properties at work in the play's opening lines[67] conforms to the notion of 'doubleness' projected throughout the Lylian canon – insistently promoted through the see-saw rhythms of the euphuistic mode, the unresolved debates underpinning both plays and prose works, and the imagery enforcing the duality of the natural world.[68] As in the rest of the Lylian corpus, moreover, the paradoxical union of opposites at the heart of *The Woman in the Moon* is integrally related to the capacity for change. The inanimate images in Nature's storehouse waiting to be called by Concord and Discord into life, the 'wand'ring' (5.1.333) planets with their pre-ordained 'motions' (1.1.122), who subject the physical world to their shifting influence, the eternal deities with their mutable affections and multiple personalities (cf. 2.1.13–18 and 5.1.287–90), combine to create the sense of an unstable universe, constant, like all Lyly's play worlds, only in inconstancy, and subject to an endless process of mutation.[69] The multifacetedness and mutability that become Pandora's condition are thus at one with the variegated fabric of the universe evoked in Nature's opening speech, while the myth that Lyly structures of her metamorphosis into the woman in the moon serves to align her, and thus the female sex she ultimately governs, with the operations of the cosmos, the rhythms of nature, and ultimately the process of creation itself, in both its sublunary and its celestial dimensions.

The Lylian myth of the translation of Pandora into Cynthia's sphere enfolds yet another fable concerning not the woman but the man in the moon. Not only does the play advance 'A point beyond the ancient theoric' (Prologus, line 3) in detecting a female, rather than a male, presence in the planet, it offers a fresh explanation (as noted above) for the appearance of the figure of a man on the moon's surface, and for the thorn bush that he bears on his back. At the close of the action, Pandora's husband, Stesias, is punished for his failure to value his wife by being obliged to attend upon her, in her role as Luna, in perpetuity, while he, in turn, revenges himself on his servant Gunophilus, who has been turned into a thorn bush for his disobedience to Nature, by carrying him to the moon with him, hoping to scratch his wife's face with his thorns. The fate of the two characters contributes to the complex intermeshing of fable within fable at work in the structure of the play and literalizes the process of metamorphosis in progress from the outset of the work, affording visual testimony, in the case of Gunophilus, to the fluidity of the universe that the characters inhabit. The physical change that he undergoes looks back to those of a sequence of Lylian characters whose transformation into aspects of nature or inanimate objects evokes a world conceived in Ovidian terms,[70] and the play's closing emphasis on translation, of both place (terrestrial to celestial) and person (animate to inanimate) serves to locate the work generically in the context of Ovidian myth.

The kaleidoscopic nature of the fable enacted in *The Woman in the Moon* has given rise to a critical response to the play as shifting and unstable as Pandora herself. Just as the planets, at the close of the play, are permitted by Nature to 'glance' at the heroine in their 'aspects' in the course of their progress across the heavens (5.1.335), so the scholarly community have surveyed her career from different angles, and constructed her story in different ways. Whereas for

E. C. Wilson, for example, the play is 'an unreserved satire of women',[71] for David Bevington, its tenor is 'not necessarily misogynistic',[72] while to Maurice Charney, Pandora's declarations at the play's 'triumphant' close 'sound like an early feminist manifesto'.[73] The character of the central figure is equally a matter of dispute. To Anne Lancashire she is 'unlikable and helpless',[74] for Michael Pincombe the source of Utopia's corruption,[75] while to G. Wilson Knight she is 'the prototype of Shakespeare's Cleopatra',[76] and for Maurice Charney a model for Shakespeare's heroines in her 'irrepressible charm'.[77] No agreement exists, moreover, on either the tone of the play or the generic category to which it belongs. To W. W. Greg 'its utilization of mythological material, bears a distinct relationship to the masque', while its 'satirical conception and representation of womankind' give the work its 'tone'[78] – a position 'emphatically' repudiated by Hunter who sees satire as essentially incompatible with the play's 'pastorally poetic and pageant-like' concerns.[79] And whereas for Bevington the work constitutes 'a melancholy instance of an image tarnished and a vision lost',[80] for Lancashire it is 'the supreme pastoral compliment to Elizabeth'.[81]

The generic instability of the work and its capacity to yield contrary meanings accords with the self-conscious extension of formal boundaries characteristic of Lyly's other late plays,[82] and the self-proclaimed evasiveness of the corpus as a whole. The elusiveness of the meaning of the myth enacted in the course of the drama, and implicit (as noted above) in its title, is summed up in the (slightly modified) address to the audience prefacing the first scene of the companion play: 'We hope in our times none will apply pastimes, because they are fancies; for there liveth none under the sun that knows what to make of the [Wo]man in the Moon. We present neither comedy, nor tragedy, nor story, nor anything, but that whosoever heareth may say this: "Why, here is a tale of the [Wo]man in the Moon".'[83]

TOPICAL APPLICATION

One of the central issues dividing critics of *The Woman in the Moon* is the application of the work to the Elizabethan court. Of Lyly's eight surviving plays all but *Love's Metamorphosis* and *Mother Bombie* were performed before the Queen, and there is evidence to suggest that *Love's Metamorphosis* may also have been designed for the monarch's entertainment.[84] *Campaspe, Sappho and Phao, Galatea,* and *Endymion* are all prefaced by prologues overtly addressed to their principal spectator,[85] and figures representative of some aspect of the sovereign appear throughout the corpus. Alexander, in *Campaspe,* for example, reflects Elizabeth in his ambition to create a state that excels in both arms and arts, while the heroine of *Sappho and Phao,* like the virgin queen herself, is torn between her private affections and her duties as head of state. A female ruler or authority figure, surrounded by a group of ladies or nymphs, appears in a number of the plays (e.g. *Sappho and Phao, Galatea, Endymion*), and identification with the circle outside the world of the drama is encouraged by the use of the classical names under which the monarch is celebrated in sixteenth-century court panegyric (e.g. Diana in *Galatea,* Cynthia in *Endymion*). The plays invariably turn on issues of direct relevance to the Elizabethan court (e.g. the conflict between love and chastity, and the proper role of the courtier), and direct references to contemporary affairs are not difficult to locate. *Midas,* for example, presents a transparent allegory of the errors of judgement of Philip II of Spain, and includes a lengthy encomium on Elizabeth shadowed under the person of the Prince of Lesbos (3.1.1–72).

Lyly's avowed innocence of topical intent, moreover, serves, paradoxically, to promote audience awareness of the plays' proximity to the world they address, inviting the discovery of 'masked contemporary meanings'.[86] The epilogue to *Sappho and Phao,* for example, expresses the hope that nothing will be 'misconstrued' by the 'deep insights' (line 14) of the spectators, while the prologue to *Endymion* claims that the work is a fiction, and should consequently be exempt from the (implicitly hostile) attentions of those engaged in the attempt to 'apply pastimes' (lines 7–8). The 'application' of the plays to both sixteenth-century politics and the career of the dramatist himself has consequently been a major preoccupation of Lylian studies, though commentators have not always agreed on the meanings figured in the works. A representation of the Duc d'Alençon, for example, in the person of Phao in *Sappho and Phao* has been both discovered and discounted,[87] and the title figure of *Endymion* has been identified, with varying degrees of confidence, with the Earl of Leicester, the Earl of Oxford, and the dramatist himself.[88] While differing over the precise historical circumstances to which the comedies allude, however, commentators have rarely dissented from

the proposition that the central female characters reflect in some
way on the Queen, and have generally concurred with Wilson
Knight's assertion that 'Lyly's plays more precisely than any others
reflect the court of Elizabeth'.[89]

The Woman in the Moon conforms in large measure to the para-
digm of Lylian comedy outlined above. The title-page indicates that
the work was performed at court; both the presiding deity and the
central figure are female; and the play's principal authority figure is
attended by two handmaids, who wait upon her will. The drama is
prefaced by a Prologue disclaiming any serious intent (cf. the equation of the work with a 'dream', lines 12 and 17), while the name of
the central figure invites identification with the monarch, in that
'Pandora' is among the names used by court poets with reference
to the Queen.[90] William Warner, for example, in his *First and Second
Parts of Albion's England* (1589, reprinted 1592), a work roughly contemporary with *The Woman in the Moon*, refers to Elizabeth as 'our
now *Pandora*' (bk 6, chap. xxxiii, line 57), while George Peele, in
Descensus Astraeae (1591), includes 'Pandora' in a list of the names
under which the monarch was celebrated (cf. 'Our faire Astraea, our
Pandora faire, / Our faire Eliza, or Zabeta faire': lines 40–1).[91]
George Whetstone, moreover, anticipates Lyly in rewriting Hesiod's
misogynistic myth in his lines celebrating 'the *excellencie* [my italics]
of PANDORA' (i.e. Elizabeth) prefacing the second part of his *An
heptameron of ciuill discourses* (1582). Concerned at the destruction
wrought by his anger at men's sins, Jove sends a messenger to earth
with gifts from the gods, who sees 'a Queene, crownd with the
worlds renowne', to whom he gives 'Faire PALLAS forme, and
VENVS louely face: / Sweete PITHOS tongue, and DIANS chaste
consent: / And of these giftes, PANDORA nam'd her Grace' (A3r)
– compare *The Woman in the Moon*, 1.1.95–104.

The implied invitation to 'apply' the action of the play, extended
in *The Woman in the Moon* by the familiarity of the Lylian formula
and the name of the title figure, is complicated, however, by both
the character of the heroine and the process that the drama enacts.
Though Pandora is not ultimately responsible for her actions (see
pp. 20–1 above), she nevertheless becomes temperamentally unstable, fickle in her affections, mendacious, and ultimately mad, while
the play traces the course of events by which the female sex as a
whole becomes 'mutable in all their loves, / Fantastical, childish, and
foolish in their desires, / . . . / And stark mad when they cannot have
their will' (5.1.329–32). The tenor of the piece is thus at a consid-

erable remove from the eulogistic vein of Elizabethan panegyric, and the work has consequently proved difficult to accommodate within the spectrum of sixteenth-century court drama designed to celebrate the virtues of the Queen. As Bond notes, 'if personal allegory exists in this play, it is satirical rather than complimentary'[92] but, though Albert Mézières in 1863[93] was prepared to read the play as an outright attack on the monarch prompted by her avarice, few critics have found themselves able unequivocally to endorse that position. Bond acknowledges that the question of the play's application to the monarch is 'very difficult to decide' and notes that though 'it is not impossible' it is 'inconsistent' with the dramatist's 'expectations of royal favour'.[94] Similarly E. C. Wilson confesses his 'inability to fathom the exact intent of this unreserved satire of women', and describes the play as 'an amazingly stupid move for favor if Lyly was still seeking advancement' and as a 'most reckless [one] if he was determined to speak out in anger at lack of desired reward'.[95] For Hunter the notion that Pandora reflects Elizabeth 'should be too absurd to require refutation', implying 'a general migration of *lunacy* out of the play and into the author, the master of the Revels, the licenser for the press, the actors and the worshipful company of stationers'.[96] More recent commentators, however, have been less ready to discount altogether the notion that the play bears witness to Lyly's disillusion with the late Tudor court. Though Pincombe, for example, concedes that 'it seems entirely unlikely that Lyly is alluding to Elizabeth specifically in his portrait of Pandora', he is ready to admit the possibility that he is glancing at 'Eliza', the monarch's literary alter ego, and that though Pandora is 'primarily a figure of Lyly's own Muse' she may also 'have been informed by a sense of general *rassentiment* against the queen . . . or, more generally, at the constraints of royal service'.[97]

'Good allegory', however, as Bevington reminds us, 'should lend itself to supple and complex interpretation',[98] and Lylian drama characteristically fulfils this requirement, rarely lending itself to explication in terms of a one-to-one correlation between actuality and fiction,[99] as the difficulty of identifying the historical figures the plays allude to confirms. Structured in terms of a 'labyrinth of conceits',[100] the comedies generate multiple meanings and explore aspects of court life from a variety of perspectives, rather than simply eulogising the sovereign, like Whetstone's *Heptameron* or Peele's *Descensus Astraeae*, under a mythological pseudonym. In the case of *The Woman in the Moon*, though the use of the name Pandora encourages identification with the Queen, the heroine's position as Nature's prime creation at once aligns her with, and distances her from, the play's principal spectator, in that for all her endowments she is not an authority figure, and it is authority figures in Lylian drama who principally reflect on the monarch. In *Campaspe*, for example, it is Alexander who is faced with decisions that bear on the responsibilities of those in positions of power, while in *Sappho and Phao* it is the Princess of Syracuse who finds herself torn between her public duties and her private affections. In *The Woman in the Moon*, it is Nature who both initiates and determines the outcome of the action, and her dominant position in the play world is signalled by the fact that she enters with attendants, and by the telling announcement that she is 'only Queen' (Prologue, line 6).

The very extent of the powers Lyly attributes to Nature encourages the construction of the work, not as an indictment of Elizabeth, but as the dramatist's fullest celebration of his sovereign in her role as head of state. Rather than being an instrument of the gods, 'lovely' Nature is all-powerful, engaged in 'glorious work' that excites the 'envy' of lesser agencies, who are nevertheless obliged to bow to her 'doom' (Prologue, lines 6–10). It is she who brings together the conflicting tendencies of her world to create a new order (1.1.25–9), imposes her will on both male and female powers seeking to exert their authority in opposition to her wishes (1.1.118–29), and she who bestows blessings and breathes life into those in her service (1.1.51–74). At the same time, however, Pandora, her supreme earthly creation, may figure a different aspect of the monarch (compare the representation of Elizabeth in *Midas* as both Sophronia and the Prince of Lesbos).[101] Not only does the heroine's name suggest identification, on some level, with the Queen as noted above, but Nature accepts the mutable central figure as her own (cf. 'my Pandora', 5.1.292), implying an intimate relationship or bond between the two. Where divine Nature embodies the public role or office of the monarch, the earthly Pandora may be designed to shadow her private identity – her multiplicity of gifts, her shifting purposes dictated by external forces, and the Cleopatra-like fascination exerted by her over the members of her court. The play may thus be seen as presenting neither an idealized portrait of 'England's Eliza' nor a satirical representation of her flaws, but a multifaceted image of the monarch's public and private selves, with the mutability of the latter sublimated through the agency of the former at the close, and assimilated to the workings of celestial powers.[102] Rather than constituting an impolitic attack on the sovereign, *The Woman in the Moon* may thus be aligned with the broad spectrum of Lylian comedy in engaging in a species of debate,[103] turning in this instance on the familiar sixteenth-century topic of the ruler's divided self, and offering a mythical enactment of the process by which the mundane qualities of one personality are transmuted (in the person of Cynthia) into the transcendence of the other.

A rather different argument for the play as homage rather than satire may be adduced from the circumstances in which it was performed. Arguing that the key to one interpretation of the play is to align it 'in historical time' with 'pastoral entertainments centred on [the] Queen',[104] Lancashire suggests that the monarch in her 'canopied chair of state', situated 'either beside the throne of the gods or opposite it', was equated at the first performance of the work not with Nature or Pandora but with 'the influential planets/pagan deities', and that as 'a constant *one* to their episodic sequence of seven', she became, as the play moved forward, 'a stable alternative to their variety, a point of constancy in an inconstant world'. In this reading of the play, the 'inclusive staging' of court drama results in the aristocratic audience, centring on the monarch, becoming 'the ordered, golden ideal: court over country, art over nature, masque over antimasque, Christianity over paganism'. In short, 'Arcadia is realized only through and at the court of Elizabeth'.

Equally capable of construction as satire or celebration, *The Woman in the Moon* exhibits the instability of meaning characteristic of Lyly's work. Like the dramatist's other court comedies it presents the audience with a conundrum, a 'labyrinth of conceits' or a 'dance of a fairy in a circle',[105] and there is something 'pleasing', as Wilson Knight notes, 'about our very mystification'.[106] The game on which the playwright is engaged, however, is a dangerous one to play. The multiple meanings yielded by his dramas leave them open to adverse construction, as Lyly himself is plainly aware,[107] and there is some evidence to suggest that *The Woman in the Moon* may not have been favourably received. Though, as Hunter points out (see p. 27 above), none of those involved in the production of the play would have been foolish enough to countenance an overt attack upon the Queen, it is possible that the responses of those commentators who have read the work as satiric may accord with those of the monarch herself. Lyly's promise to write more plays in verse 'unless the first displease' (Prologus, line 19) was not, in fact, fulfilled, while his hopes of preferment to the office of the Revels failed to come to fruition. The theatrical company which may well have performed the piece (see above, p. 8) was abruptly dissolved, and the play itself was not licensed for publication until 1595, and did not appear on the bookstalls until 1597. The work may thus document the decline of the dramatist's relationship with the court, and for all its success in artistic terms may have been adjudged by its author a disappointing failure.

The uncertainty surrounding the date at which *The Woman in the Moon* was composed inevitably casts doubt on every hypothesis regarding its application and its reception. The play may or may not have been written circa 1590, it may or may not reflect adversely on the monarch, and it may or may not have occasioned royal displeasure, bringing about the demise of Paul's Boys. In short, the work may be seen as a fitting climax to the dramatist's career, as his final, and most impenetrable, puzzle.

THE COMIC UNDERLING

The Woman in the Moon and *Love's Metamorphosis* stand aside from the rest of the Lylian canon in that neither includes a sub-plot which reflects on the principal concerns of the work. Throughout the remainder of the corpus, groups of apprentices, young servants, or pages lament the difficulties of their situations, mock the deficiencies of their superiors, and contribute to the instability of the worlds they inhabit through their conscious or unconscious dismantling of the capacity of language to communicate. In *Campaspe*, for example, Manes, Granichus, and Psyllus compare the disadvantages of their positions as servants to Diogenes, Plato, and Apelles respectively, and demonstrate to both the audience and their fellow Athenians that words may have 'divers significations' (3.2.24). Similarly in *Galatea*, Rafe, Robin, and Dick seek their fortunes, unsuccessfully, under a succession of fraudulent masters, discovering through them the multiple meanings of which the most familiar words are capable (cf. 1.4.32ff.). Though initially distinct in their area of activity from the main plot characters, the servant figures invariably reflect on the concerns of the main plot group, offering a comic perspective on the events of the play. Robin, Rafe, and Dick, for example, are engaged, like their social superiors, in some process of transformation,[108] while the pages of *Midas* offer a running commentary through their activities 'on the absurdities of courtly competition and self-promotion'.[109] In the course of Lyly's career, moreover, the sub-plot figures come into progressively closer contact with the members of the main plot group. Whereas in *Galatea*, the would-be apprentices have no influence over their succession of masters and encounter the principal characters only in the closing scene of the play, in *Endymion* the diminutive pages attempt to gain access to the title figure as he lies asleep on the lunary bank, and the young servants of *Mother Bombie* are actively enlisted by their less intelligent masters to promote their marital designs.

Gunophilus, in *The Woman in the Moon*, is clearly the direct descendant of the nimble-witted underlings of previous plays. He is sent by Nature to serve Pandora (1.1.150–5), grumbles at the reception accorded to him by his mistress (1.1.167–70), comments wryly on the action (e.g. at 1.1.212–16), and exhibits a fuller understanding than his social superiors of the situations that Pandora promotes (e.g. at 4.1.242–5). His youth is indicated by references to him as a 'youngling' (5.1.152), and as a 'lad' (5.1.153), and he displays the same readiness to slip into Latin as the precocious youths of earlier plays (e.g. at 3.2.260). Rather than forming part of a sub-plot group, largely independent of the principal figures, however, Gunophilus is the play's only representative of the servant class, and is fully assimilated into the drama's central concerns. Whereas the boys of earlier plays are co-opted to promote their employers' amatory schemes (cf. Epiton in *Endymion* and the servants of *Mother Bombie*), Gunophilus is wooed by his mistress, and is the first, other than her husband, to enjoy her favours. Though it is made clear in 3.2 that he has not found an opportunity at that stage to cuckold his master (lines 216–18), it is established in the same scene that he and Pandora have kissed at considerable length, and he continues to hope that she will be his throughout the remainder of the play. When Pandora transfers her favours from him to the Utopian shepherds, he plays the role of jealous lover, openly resenting their attentions to his mistress, and gleefully assisting in her schemes to engineer their undoing when they seek revenge for her unfaithfulness. At the close of Act 4 he runs away with his mistress, not as her servant but her lover, and is finally transferred to the moon in the shape of a thorn bush, to follow her in perpetuity, borne on his master's back.

Just as the complete assimilation of the comic servant into the main plot action may be seen as the culmination of a process at work in earlier plays, so too may the shift in the balance of capabilities between servant and master. Whereas Manes and Psyllus, in *Campaspe*, for example, for all the wittiness of their exchanges, simply do

their masters' bidding, and Rafe, in *Galatea*, displays his intellectual limitations in attempting to engage with the alien languages of
a variety of professions, the boys of *Midas* outwit their comic antag-
onist, while the young servants of *Mother Bombie* are the (unreliable)
agents of their intellectually inferior employers' ambitions. In *The
Woman in the Moon*, though Gunophilus is clearly established as a
comic figure, functioning as a humorous commentator on the action
throughout, he is presented as neither a fool nor a species of
grotesque nurturing ludicrous aspirations towards his mistress. It is
Pandora, as noted above, who initiates the sexual aspect of their
relationship, and, for all his unwashed hands (cf. 3.2.78–81) and
self-proclaimed fondness for wine (cf. 3.2.208–15), he is in many
ways more deserving of her than any of the Utopian shepherds who
sue Nature at the outset for a mate. Whereas Stesias, Learchus,
Melos, and Iphicles all seek to revenge themselves on Pandora for
her unfaithfulness, and repudiate her emphatically at the end of the
play, Gunophilus remains loyal to his changeable mistress (hence
the significance of his name, see p. 51n.16 below), and is still plead-
ing to be allowed to remain with her when he is transformed into a
thorn bush at the close. Unlike Iphicles and Melos, who see
Pandora's lunacy as a fitting punishment for her conduct (cf.
5.1.136–8), Gunophilus regards it as the ultimate expression of her
charm (cf. 5.1.119–23), and is more appreciative of her 'infinite
variety' than any of her other suitors. His stance is plainly not, moreover, the product of stupidity, in that it is evident that none of the
shepherds is his intellectual equal. His master, Stesias, acts on his
advice (cf. 3.2.185ff.), while he is quick to respond to Pandora's
whims (cf. 2.1.84ff.) and to grasp her devices, when the shepherds
are confused and easily deluded (e.g. at 4.1.242–5).

The most notable distinction between Gunophilus and Lyly's previous comic creations, however, lies in the underling's relationship
not with those inside but those outside, the play world. Whereas
earlier young servants engage in word games, jokes, and plots among
themselves, Gunophilus has no confidant within the world of the
drama, but establishes a conspiratorial relationship with the audience, inviting their support from the outset by wry reflections on his
situation (cf. 1.1.167–70), humorous flights of fancy (cf. 3.2.206–21),
and invitations to endorse his pronouncements (cf. 5.1.24). Though
Pandora is the play's central figure, it is thus Gunophilus who is
foregrounded by the structure, and he, rather than the deluded
shepherds, who elicits audience sympathy, functioning as an inter-

mediary between the spectator and the play world. Though he is finally transformed by Nature into a thorn bush for failing to observe the spirit of her injunction to serve Pandora well, his earlier plea to Jove, to punish him by allowing him 'to live still' with his mistress (5.1.271–2), is ironically fulfilled, in a process that transforms his master's vengeful request to Jupiter to 'convey [Pandora] from the earth, / And punish this Gunophilus, her man' (5.1.269–70) from a punishment into an apotheosis. At the close of the play, it is Pandora and her servant, rather than the injured Stesias, bound to a fate he bitterly resents, who ultimately achieve their desires, and their unlikely alliance that engages audience support and prompts the most lyrical moments of the play (cf. 5.1.95ff.).

The metamorphosis of Gunophilus into a hawthorn may also been seen as a development of ideas at work in previous plays. From the outset of his career Lyly is concerned with the mutability of every aspect of the physical world and the corresponding instability of the realm of ideas. The plays are filled with transformations, both physical and mental, and the process of metamorphosis is frequently represented on stage. In *Endymion*, for example, not only do characters change their intentions (cf. the transmutation of Tellus' love for the hero into hate), but Endymion himself visibly ages, while Bagoa is turned into a tree. Similarly, in *Love's Metamorphosis*, Protea is transformed into Ulysses and then back to her own shape, while the obdurate nymphs, having been translated into a rock, a bird, and a flower, resume their human forms through the agency of a 'showre' (5.4.34). In *The Woman in the Moon*, the theme of change is implicit from the outset: evoked by the title, ordained by the gods, enacted through the career of the heroine, provoked by Pandora's conduct, and finally literalized in the metamorphosis undergone by Gunophilus at the close. Lyly's last comic servant is thus not only foregrounded by the play's structure, he becomes an emblem, in the course of the final scene, of the universe that the characters inhabit.

The prominence afforded to Gunophilus has given rise to some speculation that his representative status may extend beyond his literalization of the concept of change. Noting the tendency of the comic underlings of Lyly's last three plays 'to enact dramatic fictions', Alwes describes Gunophilus as the dramatist's most 'enterprising impresario', acting as 'straight man' to Pandora, promoting her 'deceptive fictions', and engaging in an 'elaborate hoax'[110] of his own (the deception of Stesias in 3.2). His position within the metadramatic structuring of the play encourages an equation between the figure and the dramatist himself, denoting a shift, in Alwes's view, in Lyly's stance towards his audience and his art. The would-be servant of earlier plays gives place here to a theatrical entrepreneur, engaged with his own 'profit or amusement' rather than the pursuit of patronage through 'courtly panegyric'. Though the degree to which Lyly may be equated with any of his characters is debatable, the contention that Gunophilus functions as a species of stage manager is beyond dispute, and his orchestration of his own and Pandora's devices, and his role in the construction of plays-within-plays, contribute to both the fluidity of the play world and the structural complexity of the piece.

DRAMATURGY AND STAGING

Though written in blank verse and informal prose, rather than the patterned euphuistic mode characteristic of the Lylian corpus, *The Woman in the Moon* conforms in its stylization to the generality of the dramatist's work. The sequential ascent and descent of the deities who dictate the heroine's moods, the group responses of the four shepherds as they 'number down the line',[111] the processes of rapprochement and alienation enacted between Pandora and her lovers, all contribute, as noted above, to that 'dance-like'[112] mode of progression and emphatic emphasis on artifice that constitute the distinguishing features of Lylian drama (see p. 15 above). At the same time, however, *The Woman in the Moon* differs from the dramatist's previous compositions in that its central figure is a more complex creation than any of her predecessors, while her servant exists on terms of intimacy with the audience unique, as previously discussed, in the Lylian corpus. Pandora's changing disposition and capacity to play parts, together with Gunophilus' confidential asides to the spectator, transforms the 'unconfiding artifice'[113] of Lyly's earlier work into a type of dramaturgy that simultaneously invites enjoyment of its pattern, while frustrating objective reflection on the abstractions explored through its design, by the complicity that it increasingly promotes as the action evolves with the central figures.

The rapid shifts of disposition that Pandora undergoes through the influence of the planets make far greater demands on the performer than any other Lylian role. In the dramatist's previous compositions the characters function as embodiments of intellectual positions (e.g. Trachinus and Pandion in *Sappho and Phao*) or behavioural types (e.g. the nymphs of Diana in *Galatea*), requiring little more of the young actors than the ability to remember lines, enunciate clearly, and contribute, on cue, to the construction of an elaborate montage of ideas. In *The Woman in the Moon*, by contrast, though Pandora's changing attitudes are externally imposed for much of the play rather than psychologically determined, the enactment of her multiple personalities demands a far greater range of performance skills than those required of a player asked to adopt or resign a single stance. Not only is she innocent, morose, arrogant, truculent, tender, amorous, and duplicitous in turn, she is assigned more stage business than any previous Lylian creation. In 1.1, for example, she '*plays the vixen with everything about her*' (176.1), strikes both Stesias and Learchus (188.1 and 194.1), refuses Melos her hand (201.1), swoons (216.1ff.), and runs away in response to the shepherds' song (224.2). In 2.1 she '*snatcheth the spear out of Stesias' hand and lays about her*' (197.1), wounds Stesias in the course of a skirmish, threatens to attack the injured man for a second time (208), and beats Gunophilus when he seeks to intervene (211 SD). In 3.2 she dances and sings with Cupid and Joculus (39ff.), flirts with Gunophilus and the three unmarried shepherds (70ff.), and speaks alternately aloud and sotto voce to her lovers both before and in the course of the banquet (230–321). In 4.1 she pretends to swoon (86 SD), to be wounded (178ff.), and to write a letter (217.1ff.), and in 5.1 she becomes lunatic, talks and behaves distractedly (15ff.), sings (80–9), and finally becomes '*sober*' (258.1) again. The impulses prompting her behaviour are increasingly located, moreover, towards the close of the drama, not in the influence of the presiding deity but in her experience in the course of the play. Her decision to revenge herself on the shepherds, for example, arises from their betrayal of her to Stesias, and is thus a product, to some degree, of her experience rather than being wholly externally imposed. Her part thus ultimately embraces 'a whole repertory of tragic and comic female roles',[114] and the versatility that it demands of the performer attests to both the dramatist's confidence in the virtuosity of his leading actor and the theatrical capabilities (if the play was indeed performed by a juvenile troupe) of the sixteenth-century private stage.[115]

Pandora is not alone, moreover, in demanding more of the actor than any previous Lylian creation. The prominence afforded to Gunophilus by the play's structure, his interactive relationship with the audience, and the succession of parts he self-consciously adopts (e.g. as the excessively deferential servant of Pandora in 2.1, as both his mistress's lover and master's confidant in 3.2, and the agent of the shepherds' deception in 4.1) all demand a dexterity on the part of the player far removed from the ability to function as an element in a design, unstable only in its shifting alignment with others. While the governing deity and the statuesque planets, reminiscent of the two-dimensional roles of the dramatist's earlier plays, evoke the timeless interplay of superhuman forces, Pandora and Gunophilus draw the audience closer, through their adaptability, to the shifting purposes of the everyday, requiring a measure of psychological credibility from the performer unique in the Lylian corpus.

The wider range of histrionic skills demanded by the work is implicit in its greater reliance on significant spectacle and the deft management of props. Whereas, in the majority of Lyly's comedies, the action moves between a limited number of antithetical locations,[116] is economical in its use of theatrical devices,[117] and requires the handling of a very small number of effects,[118] *The Woman in the Moon* depends much more heavily for the communication of meaning on visual signifiers of a variety of kinds. From the ascent of Saturn in Act 1, the positioning of the planets on an upper level denotes the puppet-like role that the human characters occupy in the play world, while the subjection of the shepherds to Pandora is indicated by the fact that they kneel in her presence at their first encounter (see 1.1.183.1). The transfer of authority between groups is signalled by the destabilization of these positions, and by the passage of items from one character to another. Though Jupiter initially dictates Pandora's behaviour from aloft, for example, at the opening of Act 2, his agreement to relinquish his sceptre to her enacts his surrender of the position of authority he holds, and the further erosion of his power is symbolized by the laying of the sceptre on the ground and its appropriation by the outraged Juno. Similarly, the predominance of Mars in the latter half of Act 2 and resulting dissension among the shepherds is enacted through the struggle that takes place over the boar's head, with the seizing of a spear by Pandora denoting her entry into the role of virago and heightened dominance over her lovers – one of whom, in a literalization of her impact on those around her, she physically wounds. In Act 3, the throwing down of the glasses by Gunophilus conveys his refusal to facilitate others' desires, while Stesias' descent into the cave signals his darkness of mind and subjection to the wills and wiles of his servant and wife. The letter, ring, and blood-stained shirt that pass from Pandora to Gunophilus, and from Gunophilus to the deceived shepherds, in the latter stages of the play, become an index of the duplicity of the central figure, and the destruction of the three tokens at the beginning of the final act registers the renunciation by the Utopians of their misguided amatory pursuit, and their final recognition of the deceptions practised upon them.

While stage business and the use of properties are both implicitly and explicitly choreographed, however, through directions embedded in the dialogue and specified in unprecedented detail in the quarto, the locations in which the action takes place are less precisely denoted than in the majority of the dramatist's works, and are largely lacking in symbolic value. Though the vertical axis of balcony, stage, and cave equates with a hierarchy of power in the play world, the disparate settings of the principal arena of the action (Utopia) do not stand, as in previous plays, in a conceptual relationship with one another. Whereas in *Campaspe*, for example, the workshop of Apelles on one side of the stage, with its colours and pictures, stands in opposition to the austere tub of Diogenes on the other, representing the celebration of the senses as against their suppression,[119] Nature's workshop in *The Woman in the Moon*, with its clad and unclad images, is a self-contained location which does not in itself contribute to the ideas explored in the course of the play, and which is simply revealed when the action requires (cf. *'They draw the curtains from before Nature's shop'*: 1.1.56.1). Similarly while the isolated cave of the aged Sybilla in *Sappho and Phao* occupies an antithetical position to the bedchamber of the youthful queen Sappho,[120] the cave into which Stesias briefly descends in Act 3 of *The Woman in the Moon* does not constitute one polarity in a patterned exploration of a topos or theme but functions primarily as a place of hiding, while supplying a localized realization of an abject state. The 'symbolic presentational'[121] platform of Lyly's earlier comedies, consequently gives way in his last play to a fluid, largely unlocalized arena,[122] endowed with specificity only by the announcements of the dramatis personae. Stesias indicates his arrival at the place appointed by Pandora for her assignation with Iphicles, for example, by the comment, 'This is Enipeus' bank' (4.1.298), while Gunophilus registers the distance that he and Pandora have travelled at the start of Act 5 with, 'We are almost at the seaside' (5.1.10). The play thus registers a shift on the part of the dramatist away from a type of dramaturgy rooted in the visual interdependence of character and location to a kind of composition in which it is the imaginative engagement of the audience with the action that endows the playing space with meaning.

The minimal staging requirements of the drama, reducible to some species of scaffold, a workshop, a bower, and a cave, contribute, as previously noted, to the uncertainty surrounding the provenance of the play. Though the fact that the workshop is concealed from view by curtains at the outset (cf. 1.1.56.1) may imply the use of a discovery space, the deployment of a similar device in antithetically organized scenes and more prominent situations in a number of other Lylian plays (e.g. Sappho's bed in *Sappho and Phao*) allows room for speculation that the shop was a free-standing structure, and the drama was not, therefore, reliant on the facilities of a particular space. Similarly, given the evidence that the work was performed at court, the positioning of the deities aloft and the descent of Stesias into the cave are clearly not dependent on the potentiality for multi-level staging afforded by the public stage (see pp. 6ff. above), and do not therefore exclude the performance of the play in an Elizabethan private theatre. The drama has fewer staging requirements, and hence is more readily transferable to any venue, than any other Lylian play, and is more amenable in its dramaturgy than the majority of Lyly's works to a variety of performance conditions, including the flexible staging and focus on character characteristic of the twenty-first-century stage.

Though *The Woman in the Moon* may appear to lend itself more readily to revival by virtue of its dramaturgy than many Lylian comedies, the circumstances of its initial staging may, nevertheless, militate against its recovery, giving rise to a further paradoxical aspect of the work. If its 'inclusive staging' did indeed embrace that supreme authority figure not included in the dramatis personae, whose presence in her chair of state opposite the planets endowed the drama with its ultimate meaning (see p. 29 above), the play in its entirety is now impossible to stage.

STAGE HISTORY

The title-page of the 1597 quarto declares that *The Woman in the Moon* 'was presented before her Highnesse', but neither place nor date are specified and no record exists of the play's performance at any venue during the early modern period. Though its sixteenth-century history remains obscure, however, the play may lay claim to a more distinguished theatrical afterlife than the majority of items in the Lylian canon. At least three productions of the work have taken place in modern times, all by groups affiliated to academic institutions. Of these, that by the London University Dramatic Society is the least fully documented. The production took place at the Twentieth Century Theatre in London on 26 February 1953, but it has not been possible to recover any information about those involved in the venture or the style of the piece. Happily, much more information is available about the most recent production, by Poculi Ludique Societas,[123] at Emmanuel College, University of Toronto, in February 2000. The play was directed by Ingrid Keenan, and staged in a balconied hall, permitting the gods to oversee the action from above. But for a small number of cuts, no changes were made to the text, and the actors were dressed in Tudor, rather than classical, costume. The success of the production is clear from a review in the Toronto student union newspaper, the *Independent Weekly*, which praised the 'cast's ensemble work', and commented that the performance 'buzze[d] with more energy, visual delights and genuine love of live theatre than many professional productions' (10 February 2000). The reference to the play's 'visual delights' suggests that the director was alert to the many opportunities for significant spectacle afforded by the text.

The most notable production of the work in modern times, however, took place at Bryn Mawr College at the Grand May Day celebration of 1928. The central role was played by Katharine Hepburn, then a student at the College, and Ms Hepburn's own recollections,[124] together with photographs and eye-witness accounts, afford some insight into the way that the play was performed. The production took place in the open air in the library cloisters, in front of a castellated colonnade, affording access to an inner space, reached by a short flight of steps. A log was positioned stage left, in front of the arched area, and photographs survive of a barefoot Pandora[125] in a simple white gown, sitting both on the steps (see p. v) and on the log in front of the colonnade, addressing, in the latter case, a bewildered or expostulating male character (Gunophilus?) in sandals, short tunic (edged with a Greek key-stone design), and Phrygian cap. A stool was positioned within the recessed area, upon which a female character (possibly Venus or Luna) was seated at some point in the play, suggesting that the gods may have overseen the action from this position, rather than from the crenellations above.[126] No obvious provision is evident in the photographs for the cave into which Stesias descends in Act 3, but an area stage left of the platform within the recess may have afforded a place of concealment. The most memorable part of the production for the spectators, however, appears to have been the spectacle of the young Katharine Hepburn curled, presumably at the close of the action, in an on-stage moon,[127] situated at ground level, and constructed in the shape of a hoop. The dimensions permitted her to lean backwards in the arch of the structure, with her feet inside the frame, creating the illusion that she was seated within the curve of the crescent – a stage picture that remained vivid in the memory of at least one member of the audience for over seventy years. The 'vivacity and charm'[128] Hepburn brought to the role, together with the entrancing nature of the effects, suggest that this Pandora was neither a helpless puppet nor the unlikeable vehicle for a satirical attack on the female sex. As the first performance of the play in modern times, the production attracted considerable 'highbrow interest',[129] and was apparently 'a tremendous success'.[130] Hepburn herself regarded Pandora as 'a great part . . . warlike under Mars. Loving under Venus . . . Funny, tearful, etc'.[131] It is hard to imagine a more distinguished successor to the accomplished young actor who first undertook the role.

THIS EDITION

As noted above, *The Woman in the Moon* appeared in only one early edition, the quarto of 1597, which forms the basis of the present text. Only three editions of the play have subsequently been published: an old spelling edition by F. W. Fairholt (1858), the monumental old spelling edition by R. W. Bond (Oxford, 1902), and a lightly annotated modern spelling edition by Carter A. Daniel (Lewisburg, 1988). All three have been collated for the present volume, and variant readings recorded in the notes. Though direct indebtedness to the work of previous editors is acknowledged in the commentary, it is impossible to note the innumerable instances in which their decisions or sensitive observations have informed the choices made here.

The play is edited in accordance with the practices set out in the General Editors' preface.

NOTES

1 Greg, i, p. 12.
2 *Ibid.*, iii, p. 1590. The ornament has been identified as the right hand side of compartment 213, described as 'a compartment of delicate

scrolls and spirals' (R. B. McKerrow and F. S. Ferguson, *Title-page Borders used in England and Scotland 1485–1640* (1932).

3 See Greg, iv, p. 1671, who assigns the work (following the Pforzheimer catalogue) to White, and *STC*, iii, pp. 155 and 290. The first volume of *STC* assigns the work incorrectly to J. Roberts.

4 *Two Learned and Godly Sermons* by Richard Greenham, printed by White and Simson in 1595.

5 A lower rather than an upper case /w/, for example, occurs at the start of lines on C3v, D3r, D3v (two instances), D4r (three instances), E3v, F1v, F2r, and F3v (two instances).

6 Errors on F1v include turned letters (three instances), misdivision of words (one instance), mistakes of punctuation (five instances), and frequent use of lower for upper case letters.

7 In the British Library (C.34.d.19), Victoria and Albert Museum (Dyce 26, Box 25/4), Bodleian Library (Malone 257 (4)), Worcester College (Oxford: Plays 3.23 (1)), Huntington Library (62382), Lilly Library (University of Indiana, Bloomington: PR 259.L9.W6), Harry Ransom Humanities Research Center (University of Texas at Austin: Pforz. 636), Houghton Library (Harvard University: STC 17090). The copy in the Bodleian Library has suffered some slight damage to the title through cropping.

8 *Campaspe* (1591), *Sapho and Phao* (sic: 1591), *Endimion* (sic: 1591), *Gallathea* (sic: 1592), and *Midas* (1592).

9 See Bevington, ed., *Endymion*, p. 3, and Hunter and Bevington, eds, *Galatea: Midas*, p. 112.

10 Bevington, ed., *Endymion*, p. 7.

11 Two ascents (those of Jupiter at the start of Act 2 and Luna at the start of Act 5) and one descent (that of Mercury at the close of Act 4) are omitted.

12 The songs first appear in the 1632 collected edition of Lyly's plays, *Sixe Court Comedies*, published by Edward Blount. For their authenticity, see Hunter, pp. 367–72, and M. R. Best, 'A Note on the Songs in Lyly's Plays', *Notes and Queries*, CCX, n.s. XII (1965), 93–4.

13 For the similarities between *The Woman in the Moon* and the rest of the Lylian canon, see pp. 4–5 and 34 below.

14 The seven planets oversee the human action, in turn, from above, while Stesias descends to a 'cave' below the site of the banquet in Act 3.

15 Hunter, p. 82.

16 *Ibid.*, pp. 83 and 82, *passim*.

17 See Scragg, *passim*, for a full discussion of the circumstances surrounding the dating of the play. Scholars dissenting from the assumption that the play was designed for an adult troupe include Michael Shapiro (*Children of the Revels*, New York, 1977, pp. 145–6), Charney (*passim*), and Lancashire (p. 50).

18 The epicene youthfulness of the shepherds is indicated at 3.1.52, when Pandora comments, 'You all are young, and all are lovely fair', and at 3.2.148–50 where she compares Melos and Iphicles to 'water nymphs', equating the former with 'Nature in a man's attire' and the latter with 'young Ganymede, minion to Jove'.

19 Joculus points to his own immaturity at 3.2.41 (cf. 'Were I a man, I could love thee') and is addressed by Pandora at 3.2.39 in terms appropriate to a young child (cf. 'pretty satyr').

20 Compare *Campaspe*, 5.1, which affords opportunities for dancing, singing, and acrobatics, and *Galatea*, 2.3, in which a group of fairies enter 'dancing and playing'.

21 The use of Latin is not, of course, exclusive to Lyly's work (cf. Shakespeare's *Titus Andronicus*). It is, however, a consistent feature of the Lylian corpus.

22 Hunter constructs these departures as evidence of 'a degree of restless experimentation which argues an author unsettled in his *metier*' (p. 83), but given the success of one at least of these plays (see Nashe's comments on *Mother Bombie* in *Haue with you to Saffron-Walden*, quoted in Andreadis, p. 18), they could equally be seen as evidence of Lyly's ability to reinvent himself.

23 At III.ii.190.1, III.ii. 203, III.ii.217 of Bond's text.

24 See, for example, Marlowe's use of the device in *Dido Queen of Carthage*.

25 Quoted in *The Rare Triumphs of Love and Fortune*, p. 37.

26 Chambers notes, for example: 'In 1582 Derby's men played *Love and Fortune* at Court, and a city and a battlement, together with some other structure of canvas, the name of which is left blank, were provided . . . The action is divided between a court and a cave in a wood, which account for the city and the unnamed structure of the Revels record' (iii, p. 45).

27 The fact that the 'cave' allows access to a position beneath the 'bower' in which the banquet takes place (cf. 3.2.185–95) is not incompatible with the argument that the 'cave' is some species of 'house'. The cave merely permits Stesias to disappear from view, and may have been incorporated into the 'bower' itself. Chambers postulates that the cave was situated over a trap (iii, p. 46).

28 iii, p. 45.

29 It may be significant that the trap of the anonymous play is associated with the diabolic, whereas the cave is a place of hiding. Lyly's cave is also associated with concealment, rather than the intervention of the forces of evil in human affairs. As Chambers notes, 'it is the mediaeval grading for heaven and hell which lies behind the Renaissance usage' of the elevated stage and trap (iii, p. 42).

30 See II.ii.456.1–2 and 462.1 (Peele, iii, p. 81).

31 For a full discussion of actor/audience interaction in sixteenth-century drama, see Anne Righter, *Shakespeare and the Idea of the Play* (1962; Penguin Shakespeare Library, 1967), pp. 36ff.

32 Compare Pandora's direct address to the audience at 4.1.127ff. in which she confides her plans to revenge herself on her lovers and invites the female spectators to learn from her.

33 See Bevington's contention that the text for the 1592 quarto of *Midas* 'seems to have been prepared by Lyly himself' (Hunter and Bevington, eds, *Galatea: Midas*, p. 112).

34 Hunter and Bevington, eds, *Galatea: Midas*, p. 4.

35 Bevington, in Hunter and Bevington, eds, *Galatea: Midas*, p. 113.

36 Hunter, in Hunter and Bevington, eds, *Galatea: Midas*, p. 17.

37 See 5.1.21 and 23nn.

38 See Scragg, *passim*, for a full discussion of the significance of the dating of the play for the construction of Lyly's biography.

39 The passage concerning Pandora is printed by Bond (iii, p. 235).

40 iii, p. 235. Bond's transcription of the pertinent passages of Fenton's work derives from a different copy of the 1567 edition from that quoted below. Though the copies differ in a number of respects, none is significant in relation to Lyly's indebtedness to the work. Belleforest's *Histoires Tragiques* itself looks back to the work of Bandello.

41 All subsequent quotations from Fenton's work are from the British Library copy of the 1567 quarto, fols 62ff. There are no substantive differences, in terms of Lyly's indebtedness, between the first and second editions.

42 A number of minor details of Fenton's narrative might also have found their way into Lyly's play. Fenton's Pandora, like Lyly's, for example, is willing to take a servant, 'the sonne of a simple artyficer noryshed in the house of her father for charitie sake onlye' (fol. 62v) as her lover; she turns from the young page to more mature lovers (compare Pandora's rejection of Cupid and Joculus as too young to interest her sexually); and is described on more than one occasion as having 'feasted' her lovers on her favours (e.g. on fol. 62v), possibly suggesting the literal banquet in 3.2 of the play.

43 The title-page reads: 'Planetomachia: / Or / the first parte of the generall opposition / *of the seuen Planets: wherein is Astronomi-* / cally described their essence, nature, / *and influence.* / Diuersely discouering in their pleasant and Tragicall histories, / the inward affections of the mindes, and painting them / out in such perfect Colours, as youth may perceiue / what fond fancies their florishing yeares doe / foster: and age clerely see what doting / desires their withered heares / doe affoorde. / Conteyning also a briefe Apologie of the sacred and mi- / sticall Science of *Astronomie:* By *Robert Greene,* / Master of Arts and Student in Phisicke'.

44 The third story is omitted from Bond's account of the work (iii, pp. 235–6), which is based on a defective edition of the text.

45 It is possible that Greene's interplanetary alliances may also find an echo in Lyly's work, in that Mars in *Planetomachia* is aware of Juno's wrongs, while Sol repudiates the activities sanctioned by Venus (cf. *The Woman in the Moon,* 2.1.162–5 and 3.2.5ff.).

46 There are also a very small number of verbal echoes that may lend support to the case for Lyly's indebtedness. Both caves are referred to as 'hollow', for example (cf. *The Rare Triumphs of Love and Fortune,* line 831 / *The Woman in the Moon,* 3.2.198), while the term 'record' is employed in both plays in the context of the happiness of lovers after a period of suffering (cf. *The Rare Triumphs of Love and Fortune,* line 1461 / *The Woman in the Moon,* 3.1.79).

47 See G. L. Brook, ed., *The Harley Lyrics* (Manchester, 1948, 4th ed. 1968), pp. 69–70. A translation of the poem may be found in R. T. Davies, ed., *Medieval English Lyrics: A Critical Anthology* (1963), pp. 71–3.

48 See Charles Elliott, ed., *Robert Henryson: Poems* (Oxford, 1963). The relevant lines read: 'Hyr [the moon's] gyse was gray and ful of

spottis blak, / And on hir breist ane churle paintit full evin, / Beirand ane bunche of thornis on his bak, / Quhilk for his thift micht clim na nar the hevin'.

49 A more favourable interpretation of the figure is that the man is Isaac, carrying the sticks for his sacrifice by Abraham. See Fairholt, ii, p. 282, where some of the tales surrounding the man in the moon are summarized.

50 Whether the figure is on or within the moon is the subject of a mock scholastic debate in *Timon*, an academic play performed at one of the Inns of Court circa 1602–3 (see J. C. Bulman and J. M. Nosworthy, eds, *Timon*, Malone Society Reprints (Oxford, 1978 (1980), lines 1808ff.), and a similar ambiguity attends Lyly's formulation, 'seated in the moon'.

51 The term is drawn from Bevington's discussion of Lyly's handling of the sources of *Endymion* (pp. 10–14).

52 For the play's application to the Elizabethan court, see pp. 24ff. below.

53 The opening lines of the Prologue to *Endymion* read, 'Most high and happy princess, we must tell you a tale of the Man in the Moon, which, if it seem ridiculous for the method, or superfluous for the matter, or for the means incredible, for three faults we can make but one excuse: it is a tale of the Man in the Moon' (lines 1–5).

54 Bevington, ed., *Endymion*, p. 14.

55 See 2.1.13–15, 2.1.47, 3.2.8–9, 3.2.110.

56 Hunter, p. 160.

57 *Mother Bombie* also departs from this formula, but it too differs from *The Woman in the Moon* in that it overtly looks back to Roman New Comedy.

58 The term derives from Barish in his seminal discussion of the pervasive ambiguity of the Lylian corpus.

59 Lyly's utilization of the protasis, epitasis, summa epitasis, catastasis, catastrophe structure of Terentian comedy is not exclusive to his later plays. See Bevington's discussion of the structure of *Sappho and Phao* in Hunter and Bevington, eds, *Campaspe: Sappho and Phao*, p. 188.

60 4.1.298–304 takes place on 'Enipeus' bank', and Act 5 in some unspecified location on the way to the sea (see 5.1.10).

61 Bond argues, in fact, that 'as regards Time, he is stricter than in any other play' (iii, p. 238). The following discussion of the play's adherence to the unity of time is indebted, in part, to Bond's account.

62 The term is drawn from Saccio, p. 203.

63 Compare, for example, Ganymede-as-Rosalind's assertion in *AYL* that once married he/she will be 'more clamorous than a parrot against rain, more new-fangled than an ape, more giddy in my desires than a monkey. I will weep for nothing, like Diana in the fountain, and I will do that when you are disposed to be merry. I will laugh like a hyen, and that when thou art inclined to sleep' (4.1.143–9).

64 Saccio, p. 202.

65 The phrase is taken from an exchange between Manes and Psyllus in *Campaspe* exhibiting the instability of meaning (3.2.16–25).

66 Though Nature, the presiding deity of the play, is female, five of the seven planets who influence the heroine are male, as are all the inhabitants of Utopia prior to the creation of Pandora.

67 Compare the shepherds who '*wanton* in their first simplicity' (1.1.4: my italics) and the '*hurtless* flames in concave of the moon' (1.1.6: my italics).

68 See, for example, the imagery of the Prologue at the Blackfriars prefacing *Campaspe*, notably: 'Basil softly touched yieldeth a sweet scent, but chafed in the hand a rank savour' (lines 14–15).

69 Compare the assertion by Tityrus in the first scene of *Galatea* that Fortune is 'constant in nothing but inconstancy' (lines 22–3), the physical and mental metamorphoses enacted in *Galatea, Endymion, Midas*, and *Love's Metamorphosis*, and the transformation in the familial circumstances of the principal characters that takes place at the close of *Mother Bombie*.

70 Compare the transformation of Bagoa into a tree in *Endymion*, the arborification of Fidelia in *Love's Metamorphosis*, and the changes undergone by the three obdurate nymphs of the same play into a bird, a rock, and a flower.

71 Wilson, p. 143.

72 *Tudor Drama and Politics* (Cambridge, Mass., 1968), p. 185.

73 Charney, 41.

74 Lancashire, p. 31.

75 Pincombe, p. 183.

76 Knight, 157.

77 Charney, 42.

78 *Pastoral Poetry and Pastoral Drama* (1906), pp. 234 and 232.

79 Hunter, p. 219.

80 *Tudor Drama and Politics*, p. 185. Compare Pincombe's view that Lyly returns in *The Woman in the Moon* to the golden age 'only to destroy it at once, in fact, only to corrupt its very being' (p. 183).

81 Lancashire, p. 47.

82 Compare *Midas*: 'What heretofore hath been served in several dishes for a feast is now minced in a charger for a gallimaufry. If we present a mingle-mangle, our fault is to be excused, because the whole world is become an hodgepodge' (Prologue, lines 18–22).

83 *Endymion*, Prologue, lines 7–12.

84 The play is closely related to *Galatea*, for example, and is described on the title-page as a 'Courtly Pastorall'. Like the majority of Lyly's plays, it was performed by Paul's Boys.

85 It is possible that *Midas* was also furnished with a prologue specifically designed for the play's performance at court since the surviving prologue is designated 'The Prologue in Paul's'. Compare *Campaspe* and *Sappho and Phao*, both of which are furnished with prologues for both private theatre and court performances.

86 Knight, 149.

87 See Bond, ii, p. 367, and Bevington, in Hunter and Bevington, eds, *Campaspe: Sappho and Phao*, pp. 165–6.

88 See Bond, i, pp. 46–7, Bevington, ed., *Endymion*, pp. 27–9, and Alwes, pp. 58–9.

89 Knight, 149.

90 A fuller survey of the use of the name in sixteenth-century court panegyric may be found in Pincombe, pp. 188–9 (n. 8). I am indebted to Pincombe's discussion for a number of my examples.

91 Peele, i, p. 215.
92 ii, p. 256n.
93 *Prédécesseurs et Contemporains de Shakspeare* (Paris, 1863), p. 70. The relevant passage is quoted by Bond, ii, pp. 256–7n.
94 ii, p. 257n.
95 Wilson, p. 143.
96 Hunter, pp. 219–20.
97 Pincombe, pp. 177 and 187.
98 *Endymion*, p. 14.
99 Even *Midas*, in which Lyly comes closest to a direct representation of contemporary figures, evades a direct equation between Elizabeth and the Prince of Lesbos, in that the idealized antithesis of Midas is a man.
100 *Sappho and Phao*, Epilogue, line 3.
101 For a discussion of Sophronia as an embodiment of Elizabeth, see Bevington, in Hunter and Bevington, eds, *Galatea: Midas*, p. 138.
102 The representation of the flaws of the monarch's private self is not exclusive to this play. Lyly's Alexander in *Campaspe* is willing to contemplate the misuse of power to achieve his ends (cf. 2.2.110ff.), while Diana's treatment of Cupid in *Galatea* verges on cruelty (cf. 5.3.91–102).
103 Compare the debate between love and chastity underlying the action of *Galatea* and choice between love and friendship faced by Eumenides in *Endymion*. As noted above, *Sappho and Phao*, like *The Woman in the Moon*, is concerned with the public and private selves of the monarch.
104 Lancashire, p. 48. All subsequent quotations in the text from this essay are from pp. 46–50. Lancashire classes *The Woman in the Moon* as among the period's 'out-and-out pastorals' (p. 22), defined as 'a work the ostensible subject matter of which is rural life in Arcadia or its equivalent, involving shepherds and their like . . . and the style of which is courtly – obviously sophisticated and contrived. Conventional motifs often found include the music competition, the wooing of a coy nymph by an amorous shepherd, the boar hunt, and the healing of a wound with herbs. The focus is on love . . . and the classical gods usually figure prominently' (p. 23). In her view, in that the genre is 'formal, stylized, highly crafted, allegorical, courtly, fashionable, intellectual, static: the pastoral was made for Lyly and his talents for it' (p. 27).
105 *Sappho and Phao*, Epilogue, lines 3 and 10.
106 Knight, 149.
107 The Epilogue to *Sappho and Phao*, for example, expresses the hope that 'nothing be mistaken by our rash oversights nor misconstrued by your deep insights' (lines 13–14).
108 For a full discussion of the relationship between the main and subplot groups of the play see my *The Metamorphosis of 'Gallathea': A Study in Creative Adaptation* (Washington, D.C., 1982), pp. 18ff.
109 Bevington, in Hunter and Bevington, eds, *Galatea: Midas*, pp. 141–2. For a full discussion of the role of the sub-plot characters of *Midas*, see pp. 139–42 of that edition.
110 All quotations from Alwes are from pp. 61–2.
111 The term is drawn from Hunter, p. 344. For an example of the technique, see 2.1.134–45.
112 Hunter, p. 160.

113 *Ibid.*, p. 159.

114 Charney, 37.

115 See Charney's contention that the role 'realizes with a rare perfection the possibilities of the boy actor's art' (*ibid.*).

116 See Bevington, ed., *Endymion*, p. 51.

117 Examples from previous plays include the network of oppositions set up in *Galatea* between a seemingly attractive group of fairies and the apparently diabolic 'black boy' who enters following their exit from the stage (2.3.5ff.), and the emblematic representation of Cupid's subjection to Diana in the same play through his broken bow, quenched brands, and clipped wings (5.3.91ff.). In *Sappho and Phao* the heroine is discovered tossing on her bed (3.3.01ff.), an action indicative of her disordered mind, while in *Endymion* Corsites is literally covered with spots to denote the spotting of his faith (4.3.42–3). The most striking visual effects in all the plays turn on some species of transformation (e.g. that of the arborified Bagoa in *Endymion*).

118 Props required for the dramatist's earlier plays include: a number of pictures (*Campaspe*); a bed (*Sappho and Phao*); a bow, arrows, and some love knots (*Galatea*); a trick tree (*Endymion* and *Love's Metamorphosis*); a stone, a stick, a set of ass's ears, and a 'tiara' (*Midas*); garlands, a rock, a flower, and a bird (*Love's Metamorphosis*).

119 See Hunter's discussion of the staging of the play in Hunter and Bevington, eds, *Campaspe: Sappho and Phao*, pp. 30–2.

120 See Bevington, in Hunter and Bevington, eds, *Campaspe: Sappho and Phao*, for a detailed discussion of the 'symmetrical opposition' at work in the staging of the play (pp. 184ff.).

121 *Ibid.*, p. 184.

122 Though the 'bower' in which the banquet takes place in Act 3 may be seen as an exception, in that some sort of 'house' is required, the structure itself does not contribute to the meaning of the work, in that it does not encapsulate a particular mental state.

123 An amateur/student group with considerable experience in the performance of medieval and early modern plays. I am indebted to the director, Ingrid Keenan, for much of my information on the production.

124 See Hepburn, p. 48.

125 Katharine Hepburn recalls that all that her father could see in the performance 'were the soles of [her] dirty feet getting blacker and blacker. And [her] freckled face getting redder and redder' (p. 48).

126 The inner space may, alternatively, have functioned as the site of Nature's workshop, or of the banquet in Act 3.

127 Mary Macomber Leue recalls that the moon was constructed of wood, painted, and approximately one board in width.

128 Mary Macomber Leue, private correspondence.

129 Hepburn, p. 48.

130 Bryn Mawr College website.

131 Hepburn, p. 48.

THE WOMAN
IN THE MOON

As it was presented before
her Highness.

By JOHN LYLY master
of Arts.

Imprinted at London for William
Jones, and are to be sold at the sign of the
Gun, near Holburn Conduit.

1597.

[Characters in Order of Appearance

NATURE,
CONCORD, } *handmaidens to Nature.*
DISCORD,

STESIAS,
IPHICLES, } *Utopian shepherds.*   5
LEARCHUS,
MELOS,

PANDORA, *the Woman in the Moon.*

Characters . . . Appearance] *not in Q; list first supplied by Fairholt and reordered and expanded by Bond. Daniel arranges names in order of appearance but describes Ganymede as 'servant to Pandora'.*

---

1. *NATURE*] the supreme deity of the play, rather than an instrument of the gods.

2, 3. *CONCORD / DISCORD*] The concept of creation as the product of opposing forces is articulated in the opening book of Ovid, *Met.*: 'For though that fire with water aye debateth / Yet moysture mixt with equall heate all living things createth. / And so those discordes in their kinde, one striving with the other, / In generation doe agree and make one perfect mother' (lines 515–18). Hence the concept of Concord and Discord as Nature's handmaids. See also 1.1.29n.

4. *STESIAS*] an attendant or person appointed or stationed to carry out orders (from Gk *stesios*, used by Lyly as a translation of the related Latin word *stator*). The name is indicative of the character's ultimate fate.

5. *IPHICLES*] the name of one of the Argonauts (also known as Iphiclus), noted for his large herds of oxen, and hence appropriate for a pastoralist. Another Iphicles/Iphiclus, the twin brother of Heracles, was (according to some sources) the first to wound the Calydonian boar (see the dispute between the shepherds at 2.1.181ff.), while another took part in the hunt.

6. *LEARCHUS*] the innocent son of Athamas in Ovid, *Met.*, bk iv, brought to grief, like the shepherds of the play, by divine malice.

7. *MELOS*] a tune, air or song (Latin). See 4.1.23–4, 55 and 186–9 for the character's association with music.

8. *PANDORA*] in classical mythology the first woman on earth, made by Hephaestus on the orders of Zeus to bring misery, through her charm, to the human race, and enriched with gifts by each of the gods (hence the name Pandora = all-gifted). The story is first related by Hesiod (*Works and Days*, lines 69ff. and *Theogony*, lines 570–612). For Lyly's adaptation of the myth, see Introduction, pp. 9–11.

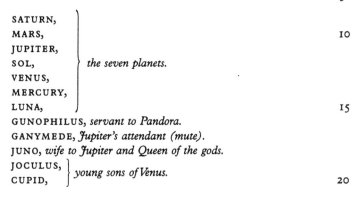

SATURN,
MARS,   10
JUPITER,
SOL,   } *the seven planets.*
VENUS,
MERCURY,
LUNA,   15
GUNOPHILUS, *servant to Pandora.*
GANYMEDE, *Jupiter's attendant (mute).*
JUNO, *wife to Jupiter and Queen of the gods.*
JOCULUS, }
CUPID,   } *young sons of Venus.*   20

SCENE: *Utopia.*]

9–15. the seven planets] According to the Ptolemaic system, seven planets
– the Moon, Mercury, Venus, the Sun, Mars, Jupiter, and Saturn (in order
of their accepted distance from the earth) – were carried around the world
by the rotation of the spheres in which they were placed, each exerting a particular influence on human life.

   16. GUNOPHILUS] woman-lover (from Gk *gune* woman + *philos* lover),
indicative of the character's devotion to Pandora.

   17. GANYMEDE] the most beautiful of mortals, known to the Romans as
Catamitus, carried off by Zeus (Jupiter) to be his cup-bearer and favourite
(see Juno's allusion at 2.1.54–5 to his distraction of Jupiter from the pursuit
of women).

   18. JUNO] queen of the gods, noted for her resentment of her husband's
numerous amours. Hence her hostility to Pandora.

   19. JOCULUS] a little jest or joke (Latin). Numerous Erotes, conceived
as young sons of Venus, accompany the goddess of love in late classical and
Renaissance literature. Joculus occurs in association with Cupid in Sonnet
LXI of Barnabe Barnes's *Parthenophil and Parthenophe* (pub. 1593), and as
a companion of Euphrosyne (daughter of Venus and Bacchus) in Milton's
L'Allegro (1632), cf. 'Haste thee nymph, and bring with thee / Jest and youth-
ful Jollity' (lines 25–6). The lines from *Parthenophil and Parthenope* read:
'Dispaire by the [*sic*] procur'd . . . leaues no roome / For Ioculus to iest with
Cupides quyuer'.

   20. CUPID] son of Venus by Mars, Jupiter, or Mercury and one of the
youngest of the classical gods. Initially conceived as a handsome youth, he
is primarily figured in Renaissance literature as a wayward child.

   21. Utopia] literally 'no place' (from Greek *ou* not + *topos* a place). The
name was coined by Sir Thomas More in 1516 as the title of his work defining the perfect society.

Prologus

Our poet, slumb'ring in the Muses' laps,
Hath seen a woman seated in the moon
(A point beyond the ancient theoric),
And as it was, so he presents his dream,
Here in the bounds of fair Utopia;   5
Where lovely Nature, being only Queen,
Bestows such workmanship on earthly mould
That heavens themselves envy her glorious work.
But all in vain; for, malice being spent,
They yield themselves to follow Nature's doom,   10
And fair Pandora sits in Cynthia's orb.
This, but the shadow of our author's dream,
Argues the substance to be near at hand;
At whose appearance I most humbly crave
That in your forehead she may read content.   15

Prologus] Q; Prologue Daniel.
1–19.] Italic in Q.
3. theoric] Q (Theorique).

Prologus] Headings, together with act and scene divisions, are in Latin
throughout, with Actus abbreviated, as in Q, to Act. at the beginning of
scenes, but not at the close.
　1. Muses' laps] domain of the goddesses (traditionally nine in number)
who inspired the arts and sciences.
　3. ancient theoric] inherited belief, i.e. the traditional explanation for the
image (held to be that of a man with a bundle of sticks on his back) created
by the shadows on the moon. Fairholt (following Grimm) notes a number
of fables relating to the figure: 'Isaac carrying sticks for his own sacrifice;
Cain, bearing the bundle of thorns unworthily sacrificed by him to the Deity,
[and] the unfortunate man who gathered sticks on the Sabbath-day, and was
stoned by the Jews' (ii, p. 282). The figure is portrayed by Robin Starveling
in MND (see 3.1.47–57 and 5.1.233–55).
　6–11. lovely . . . orb] See Introduction, pp. 9–14, for Lyly's adaptation of
the Pandora story.
　6. only] sole.
　7. mould] form.
　10. doom] judgement.
　11. Cynthia's orb] the sphere governed by Cynthia, i.e. the moon. Cynthia
(a surname of Diana) derives from her birthplace, Mount Cynthus.

52

If many faults escape in her discourse,
Remember all is but a poet's dream,
The first he had in Phoebus' holy bower,
But not the last – unless the first displease.

17.] The description of the work as the poet's dream as a strategy to fore-
stall criticism may be the source of the comparable disclaimer in *MND*: 'If
we shadows have offended, / Think but this, and all is mended, / That you
have but slumber'd here / While these visions did appear. / And this weak
and idle theme, / No more yielding but a dream' (5.1.417–22). The echoes
of Lyly's 'slumb'ring' (line 1) and 'shadow' (line 12) support the case for
Shakespeare's indebtedness.

17–19.] See Introduction, pp. 3 and 5, for the significance of these lines
in relation to the construction of Lyly's career.

18.] the first of his works composed in the realm of the god of poetry (i.e.
written in verse).

Act I

Enter NATURE, *with her two maidens,*
CONCORD *and* DISCORD.

Nature. Nature descends from far above the spheres
    To frolic here in fair Utopia,
    Where my chief works do flourish in their prime,
    And wanton in their first simplicity.
    Here I survey the pictured firmament,   5
    With hurtless flames in concave of the moon;
    The liquid substance of the welkin's waste,
    Where moisture's treasury is clouded up;
    The mutual jointure of all swelling seas,

ACT. I, SCENA I] *This ed. (in accordance with headings of subsequent acts in Q).*
0.1–2. *Enter . . .* DISCORD] *Stage directions derive from the Quarto, with editorial amplification signalled by square brackets. The following collation notes record substantive changes only, as when new stage directions or portions of stage directions have been added. The collation notes do not record routine amplifications, such as the supplying of an [Enter] where the entry is clearly implied in the Quarto by the listing of the characters names, or an [and] in a series of names. Minor departures from directions supplied by previous editors, such as the ordering of names, are not recorded.*
9. jointure] *This ed.;* Ioynter Q; jointer *Daniel.*

---

    1. *above the spheres*] above the orbits of the seven planets.
    4. *wanton . . . simplicity*] frolic . . . innocence.
    5–12. *the pictured . . . point*] a representation of the universe conceived as Nature's storehouse and compounded of the four elements (fire, air, water, earth), with all their unrealized potential (hence 'hurtless' flames). The passage may derive from Pliny, ii.iv.10–13 (see Bond, iii, p. 555), but it is possible that Lyly was thinking of Ovid's description of the 'perfect plat . . . of all the worlde' drawn by Vulcan on the doors of Phoebus' palace (*Met.*, bk ii. 7ff.) which is similarly ordered in terms of the elements.
    6. *concave*] sphere. Compare 'H. More in *Enthus. Triumph.* (1656) 191 All to the very concave [i.e. "sphere"] of the Moon' (*OED* sb. 2).
    7. *the welkin's waste*] the upper air's vast untouched regions.
    9. *jointure*] conjunction.

And all the creatures which their waves contain;   10
Lastly, the rundle of this massive earth,
From utmost face unto the centre's point.
All these, and all their endless circumstance,
Here I survey, and glory in myself.
But what means Discord so to knit the brows,   15
With sorrow's cloud eclipsing our delights?
Discord. It grieves my heart that still, in every work,
My fellow, Concord, frustrates my desire.
When I, to perfect up some wondrous deed,
Do bring forth good and bad, or light and dark,   20
Pleasant and sad, moving and fixed things,
Frail and immortal, or like contraries,
She, with her hand, unites them all in one,
And so makes void the end of mine attempt.
Nature. I tell thee, Discord, while you twain attend   25
On Nature's train, your work must prove but one,
And in yourselves, though you be different,
Yet in my service must you well agree,
For Nature works her will from contraries. –
But see where our Utopian shepherds come.   30

Enter STESIAS, LEARCHUS, MELOS, [*and*] IPHICLES,
all clad in skins.

They kneel down.

Stesias. Thou sovereign Queen, and author of the world,
Of all that was, or is, or shall be framed,
To finish up the heap of thy great gifts,

30.3. SD.] *Distinguished in Q from the majority of SDs by a change of font.*
Other examples occur at lines 1.1.56.1–3, 1.1.224.2, 2.1.202.1, 2.1.204.1.
31. SP. *Stesias*] *Fairholt (Ste.); Stosias / Q.*

10.] possibly suggested by Ovid's description of the inhabitants of the sea
depicted in Vulcan's 'plat' (see 1.1.5–12n.).

11. *rundle*] globe, circle.

13. *their endless circumstance*] the innumerable things that relate to them.

24. *makes void . . . attempt*] nullifies my endeavours.

29.] a pervasive concept in the Lylian corpus, repeatedly illustrated
through imagery exhibiting the ambivalence of the natural world. Compare
Anatomy: 'In the coldest flint there is hot fire; the bee that hath honey in her
mouth hath a sting in her tale; the tree that beareth the sweetest fruit hath
a sour sap' (pp. 68–9).

Vouchsafe thy simple servants one request.
Nature. Stand up, and tell the sum of your desire.   35
          The boon were great that Nature would not grant.
          It ever was, and shall be still, my joy
          With wholesome gifts to bless my workmanship.
Iphicles. We crave, fair goddess, at thy heavenly hands,
          To have, as every other creature hath,   40
          A sure and certain means among ourselves
          To propagate the issue of our kind.
          As it were comfort to our sole estate,
          So were it ease unto thy working hand.
          Each fish that swimmeth in the floating sea,   45
          Each wingèd fowl that soareth in the air,
          And every beast that feedeth on the ground
          Have mates of pleasure to uphold their brood.
          But thy Utopians, poor and simple men,
          As yet bewail their want of female sex.   50
Nature. A female shall you have, my lovely swains,
          Like to yourselves, but of a purer mould.
          Meanwhile, go hence and tend your tender flocks,
          And when I send her, see you hold her dear.
          Exeunt shepherds, singing a roundelay in praise of Nature.
          Now, virgins, put your hands to holy work,   55
          That we may frame new wonders to the world.

---

42. *propagate . . . kind*] perpetuate our species.
45-8.] The first of many examples of Lyly's use of syntactic patterning both within speeches (cf. 1.1.95–101) and between speakers (cf. 1.1.114–16). The device accords with the overtly structured nature of the play, and looks back to the rhetorical figures (notably isocolon, parison, and paromoion) underpinning euphuistic prose. For the use of iteration to emphasize the parallel predicaments of the shepherds (a device possibly echoed in *Love's Labour's Lost*), see 3.1.44–50 and 4.1.12–17.
48. *uphold their brood*] continue their line.
50. *want*] lack.
51. *swains*] shepherds, country folk. The term was also applied to lovers and is thus appropriate to the role that the shepherds desire and are later to play.
54.1. *roundelay*] short, simple song with a refrain. Hobbinoll recalls his pleasure in hearing the 'roundelayes' ('June', line 49) once sung by Collin, the shepherd lover of Spenser's *The Shepheardes Calender* (1579).

They draw the curtains from before Nature's shop,
where stands an image clad, and some unclad.
They bring forth the clothed image.

When I arrayed this lifeless image thus,
It was decreed in my deep providence
To make it such as our Utopians crave,
A mirror of the earth, and heaven's despite.   60
The matter first, when it was void of form,
Was purest water, earth, and air, and fire;
And when I shaped it in a matchless mould
(Whereof the like was never seen before)
It grew to this impression that you see,   65
And wanteth nothing now but life and soul.
But life and soul I shall inspire from heaven.
So, hold it fast, till with my quickening breath
I kindle inward seeds of sense and mind.
Now fire be turned to choler, air to blood,   70
Water to humour purer than itself,
And earth to flesh more clear than crystal rock.
And Discord, stand aloof, that Concord's hands
May join the spirit with the flesh in league.
                    Concord fast embraceth the image.
Concord. Now do I feel how life and inward sense   75
Imparteth motion unto every limb.
Nature. Then let her stand, or move, or walk alone.
                    The image walks about fearfully.

56.1–3. SD.] *Distinguished in Q from the majority of SDs by a change of font.*

56.1. shop] workshop.
60. *mirror . . . earth*] ambiguous. Both a glass of excellence for the human race (compare *Cym.*, 1.1.48–9) and an image of the beauty of the earth.
heaven's despite] object of heavenly resentment.
61–2.] In Lyly's version of the creation myth the first woman is created not of earth, like Adam, or from the first man, like Eve, but from the elements in their purest form.
67. *inspire*] infuse.
68. *quickening*] life-giving.
70–2.] The passage draws on the ancient theory that the human body is made up of four primary 'humours' or fluids, corresponding to the four elements. The relative predominance of one or other of the humours was thought to determine a person's physical and psychological condition – a balance of the humours constituting the ideal state. The theory is expounded by Jonson (in the person of Asper) in the induction to *Every Man Out of His Humour*.

Herein hath Nature gone beyond herself,
And heaven will grudge at beauty of the earth
When it espies a second sun below.   80
Discord. Now every part performs her functions due,
   Except the tongue, whose strings are yet untied. *cannot speak*
Nature. Discord, unloose her tongue, to serve her turn,
   For in distress that must be her defence;
   And from that root will many mischiefs grow   85
   If once she spot her state of innocence.
                              [*The*] *image speaks.*
Pandora. (*Kneeling*) Hail, heavenly Queen, the author of all good,
   Whose will hath wrought in me the fruits of life,
   And filled me with an understanding soul,
   To know the difference twixt good and bad!   90
Nature. (*Lifting her up*) I make thee for a solace unto men,
   And see thou follow our commanding will.
   Now art thou Nature's glory and delight,   → *a match for them all?*
   Compact of every heavenly excellence.
   Thou art endowed with Saturn's deep conceit,   95
   Thy mind as haught as Jupiter's high thoughts,
   Thy stomach lion-like, like Mars's heart,
   Thine eyes bright-beamed, like Sol in his array,
   Thy cheeks more fair than are fair Venus' cheeks,
   Thy tongue more eloquent than Mercury's,   100
   Thy forehead whiter than the silver Moon's.

reference to character

86.1. SD.] *Q* (*Image speakes*); *The image kneels* / *Daniel* (*with Q* / *kneeling* /
omitted from following line).
87. SP. *Pandora*] *Q*; *Image* / *Daniel*.
91. SD. *Lifting her up*] *Q. Transposed by Daniel to following l. 90* (NATURE
lifts her up).
97. Mars's] *Fairholt*; Mauors *Q*.

79. *grudge*] complain. The word recurs at line 174.
82. *yet untied*] still not loosened (ellipsis: omission of 'not').
85. *root*] (*a*) source (*b*) part of the tongue. The emphasis on female speech
as a source of mischief represents a departure from the inherited tale in
which Pandora's curiosity rather than her loquacity is the source of her
undoing. The emphasis on immoderate speech as a female failing conforms
to sixteenth-century assumptions about the nature of women.
95. *conceit*] power of thought. As the oldest of the gods, Saturn was
reputed to be the wisest.
96. *haught*] elevated (with the implication of haughty or proud).
97. *stomach*] (*a*) temper, disposition (*b*) courage.

made in the image of planets

Thus have I robbed the planets for thy sake.
Besides all this, thou hast proud Juno's arms,
Aurora's hands, and lovely Thetis' foot.
Use all these well, and Nature is thy friend,   105
But use them ill, and Nature is thy foe.
Now, that thy name may suit thy qualities,
I give to thee Pandora for thy name.

Enter the seven planets.

Saturn. What creature have we here? A new-found gaud?
A second man, less perfect than the first?   110
Mars. A woman this, forsooth, but made in haste,
To rob us planets of our ornaments.
Jupiter. Is this the saint that steals my Juno's arms?
Sol. Mine eyes? Then govern thou my daylight car!
Venus. My cheeks? Then Cupid be at thy command!   115
Mercury. My tongue? Thou pretty parrot, speak awhile!
Luna. My forehead? Then, fair Cynthia, shine by night!
Nature. What foul contempt is this you planets use
Against the glory of my words and work?
It was my will, and that shall stand for law,   120
And she is framed to darken all your prides.

claiming her

108.1. SD.] *Q. Bond supplies | During the following dialogue* PANDORA *sits apart | before Q SD.*
116. awhile] *This ed.; a while Q.*

103–4. *Juno's arms . . . foot*] all indices of outstanding beauty, echoing the Homeric epithets applied to the three figures (see Bond, iii, p. 556).
109. *gaud*] plaything, showy ornament.
110.] the biblical version of the creation of woman (see Genesis, ii.7–23), at variance with that presented in the play.
113–17.] a version of the Petrarchan 'blazon' or heraldic catalogue of a mistress's beauties. (See *Endymion*, 3.3.55–64n. for a full discussion of the device.)
114. *daylight car*] the chariot of the sun.
116. *pretty . . . awhile*] a variant of the colloquial expression ('speak parrot' or 'speaks the parrot'), commonly applied to those given to meaningless prattle (see *Endymion*, 5.4.224 and n.).
117. *Cynthia*] goddess of the moon (see Prologus, line 11n.) and hence an alternative name for Luna. Luna uses the name derisively here with reference to Pandora.
121. *framed*] fashioned, made.

Ordained not I your motions, and yourselves?
And dare you check the author of your lives?
Were not your lights contrived in Nature's shop?
But I have means to end what I begun,   125
And make death triumph in your lives' decay.
If thus you cross the meed of my deserts,
Be sure I will dissolve your harmony,
When once you touch the fixèd period.
Meanwhile, I leave my worthy workmanship   130
Here, to obscure the pride of your disdain.   *Exit.*
Saturn. Then, in revenge of Nature and her work,
Let us conclude to show our empery,
And bend our forces 'gainst this earthly star.
Each one in course shall signorize awhile,   135
That she may feel the influence of our beams,
And rue that she was formed in our despite.
My turn is first, and Saturn will begin.
                                                    He ascends.
Jupiter. And I'll begin where Saturn makes an end,
And when I end, then Mars shall tyrannize,   140
And after Mars, then Sol shall marshal her,
And after Sol, each other in his course.
Come, let us go, that Saturn may begin.

---

136. our] *Bond;* her *Q.*

122–4.] The lines are indicative of Nature's status in the play as the
supreme creator, rather than a power subject to a greater authority.
123. *check*] rebuke.
127. *cross . . . deserts*] resist that which is due to me.
129. *the fixèd period*] the predetermined limit of your sway.
131. *obscure*] dim.
133. *conclude . . . empery*] agree to show our power.
135. *course . . . signorize*] turn . . . rule.
136. *influence*] force deriving from a heavenly body, thought to determine
earthly events.
137. *in our despite*] in scorn of us.
138.1. He ascends] an emblematic representation of the planet's ascendancy (i.e. dominant influence over human affairs).
141. *marshal*] govern.

[Exeunt all the planets except Saturn.]

Saturn. I shall instil such melancholy mood
    As, by corrupting of her purest blood,   145
    Shall first with sullen sorrows cloud her brain,
    And then surround her heart with froward care;
    She shall be sick with passions of the heart,
    Self-willed and tongue-tied, but full fraught with tears.

                    Enter GUNOPHILUS.

[Gunophilus.] Gracious Pandora, Nature, thy good friend,   150
    Hath sent Gunophilus to wait on thee.
    For honours due that appertains her will,
    And for the graces of thy lovely self,
    Gunophilus will serve in humble sort,
    And is resolved to live and die with thee.   155
Pandora. If Nature willed, then do attend on me,
    But little service have I to command.
    If I myself might choose my kind of life,
    Nor thou, nor any else, should stay with me.
    I find myself unfit for company.   160
Gunophilus. How so, fair mistress, in your flowering youth,
    When pleasure's joy should sit in every thought?
Pandora. Avaunt, sir sauce! Play you the questionist?
    What's that to thee if I be sick or sad?
    Either demean thyself in better sort,   165
    Or get thee hence, and serve some other where.
Gunophilus. *[Aside]* A sour beginning, but no remedy;
    Nature hath bound me, and I must obey.
    I see that servants must have merchants' ears,

143.1. SD.] *Bond; Exeunt all but* SATURN / *Daniel.*
150. SP.] *Fairholt (Gun.).*
163. questionist] *Daniel;* Questionest *Q.*
167. SD.] *Bond.*

144–9. *melancholy mood . . . tears*] aspects of behaviour traditionally
attributed to the influence of Saturn (hence 'saturnine', having a gloomy disposition). The adverse effects of Saturn's influence are exhibited by Venus
through the 'pleasant though Tragical History' of Rodento and Pasylla in
Greene's *Planetomachia* (1585); see Introduction, pp. 10–11.
    147. *froward*] perverse.
    149. *tongue-tied*] incapable of speech.
    152. *honours . . . will*] the respect due to her wishes.
    159. *nor*] neither.
    163. *Avaunt, sir sauce*] Be gone, impudent fellow.
    questionist] disputant. The term is used contemptuously by Roger Ascham
in *The Schoolmaster* (1570) for 'scholastic philosophers, whose dialectic often
proceeded by a method of propounding and answering questions' (Lawrence
V. Ryan, ed., Folger Shakespeare Library, Ithaca (1967), p. 136n.).
    165. *demean*] conduct.

To bear the blast and brunt of every wind.   170
Pandora. [*To herself*] What throbs are these that labour in
 my breast?
What swelling clouds that overcast my brain?
I burst unless by tears they turn to rain.
I grudge and grieve, but know not well whereat,
And rather choose to weep than speak my mind,   175
For fretful sorrow captivates my tongue.
    She plays the vixen with everything about her.

  Enter STESIAS, MELOS, LEARCHUS, *and* IPHICLES.

Stesias. See where she sits, in whom we must delight!
Beware, she sleeps! No noise, for waking her.
Iphicles. Asleep? Why, see how her alluring eyes,
With open looks do glance on every side.   180
Melos. Oh, eyes more fair than is the morning star!
Learchus. Nature herself is not so lovely fair!
Stesias. Let us with reverence kiss her lily hands,
      They all kneel to her.
And by deserts in service win her love.
Sweet dame, if Stesias may content thine eye,   185
Command my neat, my flock, and tender kids,
Whereof great store do overspread our plains.
Grant me, sweet mistress, but to kiss thy hand.
    She hits him on the lips. [*He riseth.*]
Learchus. No, Stesias, no; Learchus is the man! –

171. SD.] *This ed.*
176.1. SD.] *Q. Bond adds* / *and finally resumes her seat* /.
188.1. SD. *He riseth*] *This ed.* (*also at lines 201.1 and 206.1*). *Cf. l. 194.1: He
riseth* / *Q.*

---

 170. *to bear . . . wind*] to endure philosophically every adverse change in
the weather. *brunt* = violent force.
 176.1. *plays the vixen*] acts shewishly, ill-temperedly.
 178. *for waking her*] for fear of waking her. Compare the description of
Accius in *Mother Bombie* as a spoilt son, who 'yet lies with his mother for
catching cold' (1.3.47). As Bond notes, the use of 'for' in this sense is not
uncommon in Renaissance literature (iii, p. 556).
 184. *deserts in service*] The phrase defines the relationship between the
shepherds and Pandora in terms of the servant/mistress relationship of
courtly love, with the former winning favour with the latter by accomplish-
ing her wishes.
 186. *neat*] cattle.

Thou mirror of Dame Nature's cunning work,　　　190
Let me but hold thee by that sacred hand,
And I shall make thee our Utopian queen
And set a gilded chaplet on thy head,
That nymphs and satyrs may admire thy pomp.
　　　　　　　She strikes his hand. He riseth.
Gunophilus. [*Aside*] These twain and I have fortunes all
　　　alike.　　　195
Melos. Sweet Nature's pride, let me but see thy hand,
And servant-like shall Melos wait on thee,
And bear thy train; as, in the glorious heavens,
Perseus supports his love Andromeda,
Whose thirty stars, whether they rise or fall,　　　200
He falls or riseth, hanging at her heels.
　　　　　　She thrusts her hands in her pocket. [*He riseth.*]
Iphicles. Oh, then, to bless the love of Iphicles,
Whose heart doth hold thee dearer than himself,
Do but behold me with a loving look,
And I will lead thee in our solemn dance,　　　205
Teaching thee tunes, and pleasant lays of love.
　　　　　　　She winks and frowns. [*He riseth.*]
Stesias. No kiss, nor touch, nor friendly look?
What churlish influence deprives her mind?
For Nature said that she was innocent,
And fully fraught with virtuous qualities. –　　　210

194.1. SD. *riseth*] *Q; rises / Daniel.*
195. SD.] *This ed.*
206.1. SD.] *Q; She closes her eyes and frowns / Daniel.*

---

190. *cunning*] skilful (*OED* a, 2b).
193. *chaplet*] ornamental wreath.
198–201. *as, in the . . . heels*] Andromeda, chained to a rock as a sacrifice to a sea-monster in order to punish her mother for boasting of her daughter's beauty, was rescued by Perseus who then married her (see Ovid, *Met.*, bk iv.818–906). After her death she was placed among the stars, her constellation being in close proximity to that of Perseus. Hence the notion that Perseus continues to wait upon his love.
206. *lays*] ballads.
206.1. *winks*] closes her eyes.
208. *deprives*] takes away. Compare *Luc*: ' 'Tis honour to deprive dishonour'd life' (line 1186).
210. *fraught*] filled, stored.

But speak, sweet love; thou canst not speak but well.
Gunophilus. [*Aside*] She is not tongue-tied, that I know by
    proof.
Melos. Speak once, Pandora, to thy loving friends.
Pandora. Rude knaves, what mean you thus to trouble me?
Gunophilus. She spake to you, my masters, I am none   215
    Of your company.
                    [*Pandora sinks down.*]
Learchus. Alas, she weeping swoons! Gunophilus,
    Oh, help to rear thy mistress from the ground!
Gunophilus. This is the very passion of the heart,
    And melancholy is the ground thereof.   220
Stesias. Oh, then, to sift that humour from her heart,
    Let us with roundelays delight her ear,
    For I have heard that music is a mean
    To calm the rage of melancholy mood.
                    They sing.
   She starteth up and runs away at the end of the song, saying:
Pandora. What songs, what pipes and fiddling have we here?   225
    Will you not suffer me to take my rest?   *Exit.*
Melos. What shall we do to vanquish her disease?
    The death of that were life to our desires.
    But let us go; we must not leave her thus.
                  Exeunt [*shepherds*].
                Saturn descendeth on the stage.

212. SD.] *This ed.*
216.1. SD.] *This ed.*
217. swoons] *Daniel;* sounds *Q.*
224.2. SD.] *Q (distinguished by a change of font); She starts up at the end of the song* / *Daniel.*
226. SD.] *Q; She runs away* / *Daniel.*
229.1. SD. shepherds] *This ed.; Exeunt* / *Q; Exeunt.* SATURN *descends* / *Daniel (conflating SDs at lines 229.1 and 229.2).*

---

212. *proof*] experience.
214. *Rude*] ignorant, uncultivated.
217. *swoons*] modernization of *Q* 'sounds'. Compare *England*: 'the sound of thy name doth make me sound for grief' (pp. 228–9).
223. *mean*] instrument, agent. Compare *A&C*: 'This blows my heart. / If swift thought break it not, a swifter mean / Shall outstrike thought' (4.6.35–7).
227. *disease*] troubled state, vexation.
229.2. *on*] onto.

[*Saturn.*] Saturn hath laid foundation to the rest,   230
    Whereon to build the ruin of this dame,
    And spot her innocence with vicious thoughts.
    My turn is past, and Jupiter is next.   *Exit.*

Actus primi finis.

230. SP.] *Fairholt (Sat.)*.
233.1. *Actus primi finis*] *Q; not in Daniel.*

233.1.] The end of Act 1.

Act 2

[ACT. 2, SCENA I]

Enter JUPITER [*attended by* GANYMEDE].

[*Jupiter.*] *A Jove principium; sunt et Jovis omnia plena.*
Now Jupiter shall rule Pandora's thoughts,
And fill her with ambition and disdain.
I will enforce my influence to the worst,
Lest other planets blame my regiment.   [*He ascends.*]   5

Enter PANDORA *and* GUNOPHILUS.

Pandora. Though rancour now be rooted from my heart,
I feel it burdened in another sort.
By day I think of nothing but of rule;
By night my dreams are all of empery.
Mine ears delight to hear of sovereignty,   10
My tongue desires to speak of princely sway,
· My eye would every object were a crown.

0.1. SD. *attended by* GANYMEDE] *Daniel; Daniel adds* / JUPITER *ascends* /.
1. SP.] *Bond (Iup.).*
5. SD.] *Bond.*

1.] From Jupiter [everything derives its] beginning, and everything is filled with Jupiter. Bond suggests that the quotation derives from the opening lines of a Latin translation of Aratus' *Phoenomena* included in an edition of Hyginus' *Fabularum liber* (Paris, 1578): 'A Ioue principium: quem nunquam mittimus ipsi / Infatum: plena vero Iouis omnia quidem compita, / Omnes vero hominum coetus: plenum vero mare, / Et portus. vbique autem Ioue indigemus omnes' (iii, p. 556). Robin Griffin argues, however, in a private letter that there is a stronger connection with Virgil, *Eclogues*, 3.60: 'ab Ioue principium Musae: Iovis omnia plena'. Virgil's would clearly have been the more familiar of the two works to a sixteenth-century spectator.

3. *ambition and disdain*] As king of the gods, Jupiter is associated with power and the arrogance of greatness.

5. *blame my regiment*] condemn my period of rule.

8–12.] Charney comments with reference to these lines: 'Under Jupiter's regime, Pandora becomes a little Tamburlaine, meditating on "The sweet fruition of an earthly crown" ... This is as close as Lyly comes to open parody of Marlowe's mighty line' (p. 39).

12. *would*] wishes that.

Jupiter. [*Aside*] Danae was fair, and Leda pleased me well;
Lovely Callisto set my heart on fire,
And in mine eye Europa was a gem,   15
But in the beauty of this paragon,
Dame Nature far hath gone beyond herself,
And in this one are all my loves contained.
And come what can come, Jupiter shall prove
If fair Pandora will accept his love.   20
But first I must discuss this heavenly cloud
That hides me from the sight of mortal eyes.
Behold, Pandora, where thy lover sits!
                                                    [*Discloses himself.*]
High Jove himself, who, ravished with thy blaze,
Receives more influence than he pours on thee,   25
And humbly sues for succour at thy hands.
Pandora. Why, what art thou more than Utopian swains?
Jupiter. The king of gods, one of immortal race,

---

13. SD.] *Bond.*
14. Callisto] *Bond (Calisto); Calisco / Q, Fairholt (Fairholt's reading wrongly
attributed by Bond to a battered letter in Q).*
23.1. SD.] *This ed.; Discovers himself / Bond.*
25. pours] *Daniel;* powers *Q.*

13–15. *Danae . . . Leda . . . Callisto . . . Europa*] all mortal women loved
by Zeus (Jupiter). Danae, immured by her father Acrisius, became the
mother of Perseus, having been visited by Zeus as a shower of gold. Leda,
wife of Tyndareus, King of Sparta, became the mother of Helen having been
embraced by Zeus in the form of a swan. Callisto, one of the companions
of Artemis (Diana), became the mother of Arcas, having herself been
changed into a she-bear. Europa, daughter of Agenor, became the mother
of Minos of Crete after being carried off by Zeus in the form of a bull. Lyly
alludes to three of the tales in describing the pictures in Apelles' workshop
in *Campaspe* (3.3.9–22), with Alcmena and Antiopa replacing Callisto as
further examples of the amorous nature of the gods.
    19. *prove*] put to the test.
    21. *discuss*] dispel, disperse (*OED* v. 1).
    23.1. SD. Discloses himself] Some stage mechanism was clearly
employed in production to effect the appearance or disappearance of the presiding deity (cf. 2.1.81–2). Bond proposes the use of 'wrappings' (iii, p. 557).
Other possibilities include a painted, hand-held cloud.
    24. *blaze*] glory, splendour (*OED* sb.¹ 5b).
    25. *Receives . . . thee*] is more susceptible to your guiding power than you
to his.
    26. *succour*] help. Here in the form of capitulation to his suit.

        And he that with a beck controls the heavens.
Pandora. Why then, Pandora doth exceed the heavens,   30
        Who neither fears nor loveth Jupiter.
Jupiter. Thy beauty will excuse whate'er thou say,
        And in thy looks thy words are privileged.
        But if Pandora did conceive those gifts
        That Jove can give, she would esteem his love,   35
        For I can make thee empress of the world,
        And seat thee in the glorious firmament.
Pandora. The words of 'empress' and of 'firmament'
        More please mine ears than Jupiter mine eyes.
        Yet if thy love be like to thy protest,   40
        Give me thy golden sceptre in my hand –
        But not as purchase of my precious love,
        For that is more than heaven itself is worth.
Jupiter. There, hold the sceptre of eternal Jove,
                                    [*Gives her the sceptre*]
        But let not majesty increase thy pride.   45
Pandora. What lack I now but an imperial throne,
        And Ariadne's starlight diadem?

                    Enter JUNO.

Juno. False, perjured Jupiter, and full of guile,
        Are these the fruits of thy new government?
        Is Juno's beauty and thy wedlock vow,   50
        And all my kindness trodden underfoot?
        Was't not enough to fancy such a trull,
        But thou must yield thy sceptre to her hand?

---

32. whate'er] *Daniel;* what ere *Q;* whate're *Fairholt.*
44.1. SD.] *This ed.; Hands it from the balcony / Bond.*
53. sceptre] *Fairholt (*scepter*);* sceptet *Q.*

---

29. *beck*] summoning gesture (Onions). Compare *Ham:* 'with more offences at my beck than I have thoughts to put them in' (3.1.125–6).
31. *Who*] I who.
34. *did conceive*] understood.
40. *be like . . . protest*] accords with your words.
42. *purchase of*] payment for.
47.] Abandoned on the island of Naxos by Theseus, having helped him to slay the Minotaur, Ariadne was found by Dionysus (Bacchus), who fell in love with her, and placed the crown that her gave her at their marriage among the stars.
52. *trull*] wanton, trollop.

I thought that Ganymede had weaned thy heart
From lawless lust of any woman's love,   55
But well I see that every time thou strayest
Thy lust but looks for strumpet stars below.
Pandora. Why, know Pandora scorns both Jove and thee,
And there she lays his sceptre on the ground.
        [Pandora lays down the sceptre. Juno takes it up.]
Juno. This shall with me to our celestial court,   60
Where gods, fond Jupiter, shall see thy shame,
And laugh at love for tainting majesty;
And when you please, you will repair to us. –
But as for thee, thou shameless counterfeit,
Thy pride shall quickly lose her painted plumes,   65
And feel the heavy weight of Juno's wrath.
                        Exit JUNO.
Pandora. Let Juno fret, and move the powers of heaven,
Yet in herself Pandora stands secure.
Am I not Nature's darling and her pride?
Hath she not spent her treasure all on me?   70
Jupiter. Yet be thou wise (I counsel thee for love),
And fear displeasure at a goddess' hand.
Pandora. I tell thee, Jupiter, Pandora's worth
Is far exceeding all your goddesses.
And since in her thou dost obscure my praise,   75
Here, to be short, I do abjure thy love.
Jupiter. I may not blame thee, for my beams are cause
Of all this insolence and proud disdain.
But to prevent a second raging storm,
If jealous Juno should by chance return,   80
Here ends my love. Pandora, now farewell.
        [He conceals himself from view.]

59.1. SD.] *This ed.; picking it up / Bond (following speech prefix at l. 60).*
81.1. SD.] *This ed.; Exit / Q.*

54–5. *I thought . . . love*] See Characters, 17n., for the relationship
between Jupiter and Ganymede.
    61. *fond*] (*a*) foolish (*b*) infatuated.
    63. *repair*] come.
    75. *in her . . . praise*] you diminish my worth in your estimation of her (i.e.
Juno).
    77. *beams*] rays (i.e. the influence exerted by the planet).

Pandora. And art thou clouded up? Fare as thou list,
Pandora's heart shall never stoop to Jove.
Gunophilus, base vassal as thou art,
How haps when Juno was in presence here, 85
Thou didst not honour me with kneel and crouch,
And lay thy hands under my precious foot,
> *He pours down a number of courtesies.*
To make her know the height of my desert?
Base peasant, humbly watch my stately looks,
And yield applause to every word I speak, 90
Or from my service I'll discard thee quite.
> *Gunophilus on his knees.*
Gunophilus. Fair and dread sovereign, lady of the world,
Even then when jealous Juno was in place,
As I beheld the glory of thy face,
My feeble eyes, admiring majesty, 95
Did sink into my heart such holy fear,
That very fear, amazing every sense,
Withheld my tongue from saying what I would,
And freezed my joints from bowing when they should.
Pandora. Ay, now, Gunophilus, thou pleasest me. 100
These words and curtsies prove thee dutiful.

Enter STESIAS, LEARCHUS, MELOS, *and* IPHICLES.

87.1. SD.] *Q; He bows and curtsies in apology / Daniel (following l. 88).*
91.1. SD.] *Q; He kneels / Daniel.*
100. Ay] *Daniel (Aye); I Q.*
101. curtsies] *Daniel;* cursies *Q;* cur'sies *Fairholt.*

82. *art . . . up*] For the implied SD here see 2.1.23.1n.
Fare . . . list] Do as you wish.
85. *How haps*] How does it happen (with a common ellipsis: 'How haps [it]').
87. *lay . . . foot*] a traditional gesture of fealty. Compare *Shrew*: 'place your hands below your husband's foot. / In token of which duty, if he please, / My hand is ready' (5.2.178–80).
87.1. *pours . . . courtesies*] bows repeatedly.
96. *Did sink*] Bond notes: 'either this is intrans. "there did sink", and the preceding line parenthetic (nom.abs.), or else *eyes* in the preceding line must be taken as subj. of *did sinke* [sic] as a causative verb' (iii, p. 557).
97. *amazing*] bewildering. Compare *John*: 'I am amaz'd, methinks, and lose my way' (4.3.140).
101. *curtsies*] acts of obeisance, bows.

Stesias. Now, Stesias, speak!
Learchus.   Learchus, plead for love!
Iphicles. Now Cyprian Queen, guider of loving thoughts,
    Help Iphicles!
Melos.   Melos must speeed or die!
Gunophilus. Whither now, my masters, in such post haste?   105
    Her Excellence is not at leisure now.
Stesias. O sweet Gunophilus, further our attempts!
Iphicles. And we shall make thee rich with our rewards.
Gunophilus. Stay here until I know her further pleasure.
                              [*He approaches Pandora.*]
    Stesias and his fellows humbly crave access to Your   110
    Excellence.
Pandora. Ay, now thou fittest my humour, let them come.
Gunophilus. [*To the shepherds*] Come on, masters.
                              [*The shepherds approach.*]
Stesias. Tell on, my dear, when comes that happy hour
    Whereon thy love shall guerdon my desire?   115
Learchus. How long shall sorrrow's winter pinch my heart,
    And lukewarm hopes be chilled with freezing fear,
    Before my suit obtain thy sweet consent?
Iphicles. How long shall death, encroaching by delays,
    Abridge the course of my decaying life,   120
    Before Pandora love poor Iphicles?
Melos. How long shall cares cut off my flowering prime,
    Before the harvest of my love be in?

105.] *Bond supplies* / *intervening between the* shepherds *and* PANDORA / *following the speech prefix.*
109.1. SD.] *This ed.;Turning to* PAN. / *Bond.*
112. Ay] *Daniel (*Aye*); I Q.*
113. SD.] *This ed.*
113.1. SD.] *Bond.*
114. on] *Q;* me *Bond (noting 'prob. for* one, *the compositor mistaking* me*').*

103. *Cyprian Queen*] Venus (from her birth on the shores of Cyprus).
104. *speed*] be successful (see 3.1.46 for a further example of the use of
the word in this sense).
105. *masters*] good sirs.
post haste] expedition.
115. *guerdon*] reward.
119. *encroaching by delays*] closing in on me through the necessity of
waiting for your response.

Stesias. Oh, speak, sweet love!

Iphicles.   Some gentle words, sweet love!

Learchus. Oh, let thy tongue first salve Learchus' wound,   125
That first was made with those immortal eyes!

Melos. The only promise of thy future love
Will drown the secret heaps of my despair
In endless ocean of expected joys!

Pandora. Although my breast yet never harboured love,   130
Yet should my bounty free your servitude,
If love might well consort our majesty,
And not debase our matchless dignity.

Stesias. Sweet honey words, but sauced with bitter gall.

Iphicles. They draw me on, and yet they put me back.   135

Learchus. They hold me up, and yet they let me fall.

Melos. They give me life, and yet they let me die.

Stesias. But as thou wilt, so give me sweet or sour,
For in thy pleasure must be my content.

Iphicles. Whether thou draw me on, or put me back,   140
I must admire thy beauty's wilderness.

Learchus. And as thou wilt, so let me stand or fall;
Love hath decreed thy word must govern me.

Melos. And as thou wilt, so let me live or die,
In life or death I must obey thy will.   145

Pandora. I please myself in your humility,
Yet will I make some trial of your faith
Before I stoop to favour your complaints;
For, wot ye well, Pandora knows her worth.
He that will purchase things of greatest prize   150
Must conquer by his deeds, and not by words.
Go then, all four, and <u>slay the savage boar</u>

(margin annotation: Class Comedy)

---

127. *only*] mere.
131. *should . . . servitude*] my generosity would free you from your
enslaved condition.
132. *well consort*] be a fit accompaniment of.
our] the royal plural. (Indicative of Pandora's inflated self-esteem.)
141. *admire . . . wilderness*] wonder at . . . wild, wayward character.
148. *complaints*] laments. The term also denotes a type of lyric poem in
which the speaker bewails or regrets the unresponsiveness of his love (e.g.
Surrey's 'A complaint by night of the lover not beloved').
149. *wot ye well*] be assured. (A common formulation.)
150. *purchase*] win, achieve.

Which, roving up and down with ceaseless rage,
Destroys the fruit of our Utopian fields.
And he that first presents me with his head   155
Shall wear my glove in favour of the deed.
Melos. We go, Pandora!
Learchus.   Nay, we run!
Stesias.   We fly!
                              [*Exeunt shepherds.*]
Pandora. Thus must Pandora exercise these swains,
Commanding them to dangerous exploits;
And were they kings, my beauty should command.   160
Sirrah Gunophilus, bear up my train.
                 Exit PANDORA *and* GUNOPHILUS.

                     Enter MARS.

Mars. Mars comes, entreated by the Queen of Heaven
To summon Jove from this his regiment.
Such jealous humour croweth in her brain
That she is mad till he return from hence.   165
[*More loudly*] Now, sovereign Jove, King of immortal
     kings,
Thy lovely Juno long hath looked for thee,
And till thou come thinks every hour a year.
                    [*Jupiter discloses himself.*]
Jupiter. And Jove will go, the sooner to assuage
Her frantic, idle, and suspicious thoughts,   170

157.1. SD.] *Bond.*
161.2. SD.] *Q; Enter* MARS, *to* JUPITER / *Daniel.*
166. SD.] *Bond (subst.).*
168.1. SD.] *This ed.; Re-enter* JUPITER *above, with* GANYMEDE / *Bond.*

156.] In the courtly love tradition the giving of a glove was a mark of
favour, signalling a lady's acceptance of a suitor's service. Such tokens were
often worn publicly by the lover as an indication of his favoured status,
usually in the hat (or the helmet when jousting).
   158. *exercise*] employ (*OED* v. 4).
   163. *regiment*] period of rule.
   164. *croweth*] cries out. Compare Greene's *Pandosto* (1588): 'His wife . . .
began to bee somewhat jelousse, [and] beganne to crowe against her
goodman' (Bullough, viii, p. 174).
   167. *looked for*] expected.
   169. *assuage*] soothe.

For well I know Pandora troubles her.
Nor will she calm the tempest of her mind
Till with a whirlwind of outrageous words
She beat mine ears, and weep curst heart away.

He descends [with Ganymede].

Yet will I go, for words are but a blast,   175
And sunshine will ensue when storms are past.

Exit with GANYMEDE.

[Mars ascends.]

Mars, in his seat. Now bloody Mars begins to play his
      part.
I'll work such war within Pandora's breast
(And somewhat more, for Juno's fair request)
That, after all her churlishness and pride,   180
She shall become a vixen martialist.

Enter the four shepherds with the boar's head.

Stesias. Here let us stay till fair Pandora come,
      And then shall Stesias have his due reward.
Iphicles. And why not Iphicles as well as you?
Melos. The prize is mine; my sword cut off his head.   185
Learchus. But first my spear did wound him to the death.
Stesias. He fell not down till I had gored his side.
Learchus. Content you all, Learchus did the deed,

174.1. SD.] *Bracketed material / Bond;* JUPITER *descends / Daniel.*
176.2. SD.] *Bond.*
177. *Mars, in his seat*] *Placement as Fairholt; on separate line centred as SD in*
Q.

---

174. *weep . . . away*] wash away her ill temper with weeping.
175. *blast*] wind.
181. *martialist*] person given to warfare.
182.] As Bond notes (iii, p. 557), the influence of the dominant planet is
expanded from this point onwards from Pandora to other members of the
dramatis personae. Here the aggressiveness associated with the rule of Mars
is exhibited between the formerly united shepherds.
185-7.] The competing claims of the shepherds may look back to the
similar controversy in *The Spanish Tragedy* (1589?) between Horatio and
Lorenzo over the capture of Balthazar. Compare: '*Lor.* This hand first took
his courser by the reins. / *Hor.* But first my lance did put him from his horse.
/ *Lor.* I seiz'd his weapon and enjoy'd it first. / *Hor.* But first I forc'd him lay
his weapons down' (Philip Edwards, ed., 1.2.155-8).

And I will make it good whoe'er says nay.
Melos. Melos will die before he lose his right!   190
Iphicles. Nay, then, 'tis time to snatch! The head is mine!
          [*He seizes the head.*] — *Comedy*
Stesias. Lay down or I shall lay thee on the earth.
                    They fight.

          Enter PANDORA *and* GUNOPHILUS.

Pandora. [*Derisively*] Ay, so; fair and far off, for fear of hurt!
      See how the cowards counterfeit a fray. –
      Strike home, you dastard swains, strike home, I say!   195
      Fight you in jest? Let me bestir me, then,
      And see if I can cudgel ye all four. — *humour*
She snatcheth the spear out of Stesias' hand and lays about her.
Gunophilus. What? Is my mistress mankind on the sudden?
Learchus. Alas, why strikes Pandora her best friends?
Pandora. My friends, base peasants! My friends would fight
      like men. *gendered*   200
      Avaunt, or I shall lay you all for dead.
                    Exeunt all, saving Stesias.

189. whoe'er] *This ed.;* who eare *Q;* who'are *Fairholt;* who e'er *Daniel.*
191.1. SD.] *This ed.*
193. SD.] *This ed.*
197.1. SD. *snatcheth . . . lays about her*] *Q; snatches . . . strikes all around her /*
Daniel.
200–1] *Line division as Bond;* My friends . . . pesants, | My friends . . . men:
| Auaunt . . . dead. | *Q.*
201.1. SD.] *Punctuation this ed.; Exeunt, all sauing /* Q; *Exeunt all sauing /*
Fairholt; Exeunt all the shepherds except STESIAS / *Daniel.*

189. *make it good*] uphold the truth of it (usually implying through battle
or hand-to-hand conflict).
192. *Lay down*] Put down the head.
193. *fair . . . hurt*] Bond notes: 'apparently a proverb of one who main-
tains a cautious and civil distance' (iii, p. 557).
194. *counterfeit a fray*] simulate a fight.
198. *mankind*] masculine (with the implication of an unnatural deviation
from the attributes appropriate to the female sex). Compare the derisive,
'Are you mankind?' directed towards the virago, Volumnia (*Cor.*, 4.2.16). The
unfixed nature of gender is a recurrent motif in Lyly's work (cf. the physical transformation that resolves the action of *Galatea* and the metamorphosis of Protea in *Love's Metamorphosis* into Ulysses).
201.1. *saving*] except.

Stesias. See, cruel fair, how thou hast wronged thy friend,
                    He showeth his shirt, all bloody.
    To spill his blood that kept it but for thee.
    There's my desert – and here is my reward!
    Pointing first to the head on the ground and then to his wound.
    I dare not say of an ungrateful mind,   205
    But if Pandora had been well advised,
    This dare I say, that Stesias had been spared.
Pandora. Begone, I say, before I strike again!
Gunophilus. Oh, stay, sweet mistress, and be satisfied!
Pandora. Base vassal, how dar'st thou presume to speak?   210
    Wilt thou encounter any deed of mine?   *She beats him.*
    How long have you been made a counsellor?
                    Exit GUNOPHILUS, *running away.*
Stesias. Here, strike thy fill, make lavish of my life,
    That in my death my love might find relief.
    Lance up my side, that when my heart leaps out,   215
    Thou mayst behold how it is scorched with love,
    And every way cross-wounded with desire.
    There shalt thou read my passions deep engraven,
    And in the midst, only Pandora's name.
Pandora. What tell'st thou me of love and fancy's fire?   220
    Fire of debate is kindled in my heart.
    And were it not that thou art all unarmed,
    Be sure I should make trial of thy strength.
    But now the death of some fierce savage beast
    In blood shall end my fury's tragedy;   225
    For fight I must, or else my gall will burst.
                    Exit PANDORA.
Stesias. Ah, ruthless heart, harder than adamant,

202.1. SD.] *Distinguished in Q from the majority of stage directions by a change
of font (also at l. 204.1).*
202.1. SD. *showeth*] *Q; shows / Daniel.*
204.1. SD. *Pointing*] *Q; He points / Daniel.*
205. ungrateful] *This ed.;* ingratefull *Q.*

---

211. *encounter*] cross, oppose (*OED* v. 2).
217. *every . . . cross-wounded*] scarred in every direction.
221. *debate*] physical strife, conflict (*OED* sb. 1b).
226. *gall*] thought to be the seat of rancour in the human body.
227. *adamant*] legendary stone, often associated through its impenetra-
bility with the diamond. Compare *Anatomy*: 'There is great difference
between the standing puddle and the running stream, yet both water; great
odds between the adamant and the pumice, yet both stones' (p. 98).

Whose ears are deaf against affection's plaints,
And eyes are blind when sorrow sheds her tears,
Neither contented that I live nor die.   230
But, fondling as I am, why grieve I thus?
Is not Pandora mistress of my life?
Yes, yes, and every act of hers is just.
Her hardest words are but a gentle wind;
Her greatest wound is but a pleasing harm;   235
Death at her hands is but a second life.   *Exit* STESIAS.
                                             Mars descendeth.
[*Mars.*] Mars hath enforced Pandora 'gainst her kind,
To manage arms and quarrel with her friends,
And thus I leave her, all incensed with ire.
Let Sol cool that which I have set on fire.   *Exit.*   240

                Actus secundi finis.

236.1. SD.] *Q;* MARS *descends / Daniel.*
237. SP.] *Fairholt.*
240.1. *Fairholt; Actus 2 finis / Q; not in Daniel.*

---

228. *affection's plaints*] the lamentations of love.
231. *fondling*] fool (but with a probable pun on *fond* = doting).
237. *'gainst her kind*] contrary to her nature.
238. *manage arms*] wield weapons.
240.1.] The end of Act 2.

Act 3

Enter SOL *and takes his seat.*

Sol. In looking down upon this baser world,
    I long have seen and rued Pandora's harms.
    But as myself by nature am inclined
    So shall she now become, gentle and kind,
    Abandoning all rancour, pride and rage;   5
    And changing from a lion to a lamb,
    She shall be loving, liberal, and chaste,
    Discreet and patient, merciful and mild,
    Inspired with poetry and prophecy,
    And virtues appertaining womanhood.   10

[handwritten margin note: womanly expectations]

Enter PANDORA *with* GUNOPHILUS.

Pandora. Tell me, Gunophilus, how doth Stesias now?
    How fares he with his wound? Unhappy me,
    That so unkindly hurt so kind a friend.
    But Stesias, if thou pardon what is past,
    I shall reward thy sufferance with love.   15

0.1. SD.] *Q (take); Enter* SOL, *and ascends / Daniel.*

1. *baser*] lower (but with the implication of inferior). Compare the extensive punning on the word in *R2* (3.3.176ff.).

3–9. *as myself . . . prophecy*] The attributes listed here serve to equate Sol with Apollo, the god of poetry, prophecy, and the most creative aspects of the human mind. Though his association with healing is not mentioned here, it is evident in Pandora's readiness to cure Stesias and knowledge of the medicinal properties of herbs (see 3.1.65ff.).

10. *appertaining*] appropriate to. The qualities Pandora displays under Sol's influence align her with sixteenth-century constructions of the virtuous woman.

11–13. *Tell me . . . friend*] The transformation of Pandora's language and attitudes on her entrance bear witness to the influence of the presiding planet.

15. *sufferance*] (*a*) injury (*OED* I 2c) (*b*) long-suffering, forbearance.

78

These eyes, that were like two malignant stars,
Shall yield thee comfort with their sweet aspect;
And these my lips, that did blaspheme thy love,
Shall speak thee fair and bless thee with a kiss;
And this my hand, that hurt thy tender side,   20
Shall first with herbs recure the wound it made,
Then plight my faith to thee in recompense. –
And thou, Gunophilus, I pray thee pardon me,
That I misdid thee in my witless rage.
As time shall yield occasion, be thou sure,   25
I will not fail to make thee some amends.
Gunophilus. I so content me in this pleasant calm,
    That former storms are utterly forgot.

> *Enter [the] four shepherds. [*STESIAS *stands apart.*
>   *The rest kneel.*]

Learchus. We follow still in hope of grace to come.
Iphicles. Oh, sweet Pandora, deign our humble suits.   30
Melos. Oh, grant me love, or wound me to the death.
Pandora. Stand up. Pandora is no longer proud,
    But shames at folly of her former deeds.

---

17. thee] *Bond;* their *Q.*
28.1–2. SD. *Enter . . . kneel*] *Bracketed material this ed.; Enter foure shepherdes
/ Q; Enter* LEARCHUS, IPHICLES, MELOS *and* STESIAS / *Daniel.*

---

16. *malignant stars*] planets exerting a baleful influence. Compare *1H6*: 'O
malignant and ill-boding stars' (4.4.6). The comparison ('like two . . .') is
unwittingly ironic in that Pandora's previous conduct was, in fact, governed
by malign planetary influence, while the 'sweet aspect' (line 17) she now
intends to turn upon Stesias is again dictated by a heavenly power.
  19. *speak thee fair*] talk kindly to you.
  21. *recure*] make well. Compare *Anatomy*: 'The filthy sow when she is sick
eateth the sea-crab and is immediately recured' (p. 54). See 5.1.212 for a
further example of the use of the word.
  24. *misdid . . . rage*] did ill to you in my unreasoning fury.
  28.1–2. STESIAS . . . kneel] The postures and relative positions of the characters may be inferred from line 32 and lines 34–5. The injunction 'Stand
up' indicates that three of the shepherds have knelt, while the question 'why
stands?' suggests that Stesias remains standing. The injunction 'Draw near'
(line 35) implies that he is at a distance from the rest.
  30. *deign*] condescend to accept. Compare *Gent*: 'I fear my Julia would
not deign my lines / Receiving them from such a worthless post' (1.1.150–1).
  33. *shames*] is ashamed (*OED* v. 1). Compare *Mac*: 'I shame / To wear a
heart so white (2.2.63–4).

But why stands Stesias like a man dismayed?
Draw near, I say, and thou, with all the rest,   35
Forgive the rigour of Pandora's hand,
And quite forget the faults of my disdain.
Now is the time, if you consent all four,
Wherein I'll make amends for old offence.
One of you four shall be my wedlock mate,   40
And all the rest my well-belovèd friends.
But vow you here, in presence of the gods,
That when I choose, my choice shall please you all.
Stesias. Then make I vow by Pallas, shepherds' queen,
That Stesias will allow Pandora's choice.   45
But if he speed that less deserves than I,
I'll rather die than grudge or make complaint.
Melos. I swear the like, by all our country gods!
Iphicles. And I, by our Diana's holy head!
Learchus. And I, by Ceres and her sacred nymphs!   50

---

44. Pallas, shepherds' queen] *This ed.; Pallas* shepherds Queene *Q; Pallas'*
shepherd's queene *Fairholt;* Pallas' shepherd's queen *Daniel.*
49. Diana's] *Daniel;* Dianes *Q;* Dianaes *Fairholt.*

---

34. *dismayed*] deprived of moral courage at the sight of danger (*OED*
v. 1).
40. *wedlock mate*] partner in marriage.
42. *in presence . . . gods*] a further instance of dramatic irony, in that
Pandora is unaware of Sol's literal presence.
44. *Pallas, shepherds' queen*] unpunctuated in Q and capable of more than
one meaning. Either Stesias makes his vow by Pallas Athena and 'shepherds'
queen' is addressed to Pandora, or 'shepherds' queen' qualifies Pallas Athena
(patroness of agriculture). Daniel's punctuation, 'Pallas' shepherd's queen',
is difficult to interpret.
45. *allow*] approve. Compare *England*: 'Unto thee I will reveal more than
either wisdom would allow or my modesty permit' (p. 219).
48. *our country gods*] gods of our country (i.e. native deities).
50. *Ceres . . . nymphs*] As Bond notes, the reference to the nymphs of
Ceres (goddess of agriculture), who do not figure in classical mythology, may
suggest that the play was composed soon after *Love's Metamorphosis*, in which
the nymphs play a central part (iii, p. 557). The fact that Ceres is accompanied by nymphs in the entertainment presented for the Queen at Bisham in
1592 may support the case for Lyly's authorship of that work, and thus his
involvement in courtly entertainments after the closure of Paul's Boys. The
uncertainty surrounding the date of composition of *Love's Metamorphosis*,
however, leaves open the possibility that the entertainment was influenced
by the play rather than being by Lyly himself.

Pandora. Then Love and Hymen bless me in my choice.
You all are young, and all are lovely fair,
All kind, and courteous, and of sweet demean,
All right and valiant, all in flowering prime;
But since you grant my will his liberty,   55
Come, Stesias, take Pandora by the hand,
And with my hand I plight my spotless faith.
Stesias. The word hath almost slain me with delight.
Learchus. The word with sorrow killeth me outright. — *humour*
Melos. Oh, happy Stesias! But unhappy me!   60
Iphicles. Come, let us go and weep our want elsewhere.
Stesias hath got Pandora from us all.
                    Exeunt [LEARCHUS, MELOS, *and* IPHICLES].
Pandora. Their sad depart would make my heart to earn,
Were not the joys that I conceive in thee.
Go, go, Gunophilus, without delay,   65
Gather me balm and cooling violets,
And of our holy herb nicotian;
And bring withal pure honey from the hive,
That I may here compound a wholesome salve
To heal the wound of my unhappy hand.   70

62.1. SD.] *Bracketed material* / *Bond.*
63. earn] *Q (*earne*); yearn *Daniel.*
68. withal] *This ed.;* with all *Q;* withall *Fairholt.*

51. *Hymen*] the god of marriage.
53. *demean*] demeanour.
54. *right*] disposed to do what is good and just (*OED* a. II. 5).
55. *grant my will his liberty*] allow my will freedom of choice.
61. *want*] lack.
63. *earn*] grieve. The word is used in the context of a deeply troubling situation in *Mother Bombie:* compare, 'My verie bowels earned within me, that I shuld be author of such vilde incest' (5.3.297–8).
64. *Were not*] were it not for.
66. *cooling violets*] The medicinal properties of the violet are widely noted and include efficacy as an opiate, a laxative, and an expectorant. The association with cooling may arise from the fact that the plant grows in the shade.
67. *nicotian*] the tobacco plant (from Jacques (or Jean) Nicot, French ambassador to Portugal, who introduced the plant into France in 1560), highly valued for its curative properties. Fairholt notes that 'the "tabaco of Trinidada" is termed *Sana Sancta Indorum,* in Gerard's *Herball,* 1597' (ii, p. 280).
68. *honey*] valued for countering infection in the treatment of wounds.
70. *of*] inflicted by.

Gunophilus. I go.   [*Exit.*]
Stesias. Blest be the hand that made so happy wound,
          For in my sufferance have I won thy love.
          And blessèd thou that, having tried my faith,
          Hast given admittance to my heart's desert.   75
          Now all is well, and all my hurt is whole,
          And I in paradise of my delight.
          Come, lovely spouse, let us go walk the woods,
          Where warbling birds record our happiness,
          And whistling leaves make music to our mirth,   80
          And Flora strews her bower to welcome thee.
Pandora. But first, sweet husband, be thou ruled by me.
          Go make provision for some holy rites,
          That zeal may prosper our new-joinèd love,
          And by and by myself will follow thee.   85
Stesias. Stay not, my dear. For in thy looks I live.   *Exit.*
Pandora. I feel myself inspired, but wot not how,
          Nor what it is, unless some holy power.
          My heart foretells me many things to come,
          And I am full of unacquainted skill,   90
          Yet such as will not issue from my tongue,
          But, like Sybilla's golden prophecies,

---

71. SD.] *Bond.*
85. follow] *Fairholt;* follw *Q.*
92. Sybilla's] *Daniel; Siballaes / Q; Sibillaes / Bond.*

---

79. *record*] warble, sing about. Compare *Gent:* 'the nightingale's com-
plaining notes / Tune my distresses, and record my woes' (5.4.5–6). Lyly uses
the term in the context of a lover's story in *England* (p. 205).
  81. *Flora*] goddess of the spring, associated with sexual love, positioned
by Lyly in opposition to Diana in defining the sexual licence of Naples in
Anatomy (pp. 33–4). The virtuous nature of Pandora under the influence of
Sol is indicated by her desire to place the fulfilment of her relationship with
Stesias in a religious context (see lines 83–4).
  84. *zeal*] fervent religious devotion.
  90. *unacquainted*] unfamiliar, strange. Compare 'What unacquainted
thoughts are these' (*Sappho and Phao*, 2.4.1) in the context of a sudden subjection to an inappropriate passion, and 'This unacquainted and most unnatural practice' (*Endymion*, 5.4.47–8) with reference to a witchcraft plot.
  92–5.] The comparison relates to the Sybil of Cunae, a fifth-century
prophetess and priestess of Apollo, who offered to sell nine books of
prophecy to King Tarquin, who twice refused her on the grounds of price.
With each refusal the Sybil burned three of the books. Tarquin finally bought
the last three books, thought to be of such value they were subsequently

Affecting rather to be clad in verse
(The certain badge of great Apollo's gift)
Than to be spread and soiled in vulgar words.   95
And now, to ease the burden of my bulk,
Like Sybil, thus Pandora must begin.

Enter STESIAS.

[*Stesias.*] Come, my Pandora, Stesias stays for thee.
Pandora. Peace, man. With reverence hear and note my words,
    For from Pandora speaks the laureate god: 100
        Utopiae Stesias phoenici solvit amorem,
        numina caelorum dum pia praecipiunt.
    And backward thus the same, but double sense:
        Praecipiunt pia dum caelorum numina, amorem
        solvit phoenici Stesias Utopiae.   105
        He, soberly repeating these verses, first forward and then
                                        backward, sayeth:
Stesias. If 'solvere amorem' signify 'to love',
    Then means this prophecy good to Stesias.

---

98. SP.] *Fairholt (Ste.).*
104. *caelorum*] Q *(celorum).*
105.1-2. SD.] *Q (not in italics);* STESIAS *soberly repeats these verses, first forward and then backward / Daniel (also at l. 115.1).*

---

housed in the Capitol. Another tradition relates that the Sybil placed the leaves of her prophecies in the mouth of her cave and that they were scattered by the wind – hence their fragmentary and enigmatic nature. The story of the unhappy outcome of her relationship with Apollo is related in *Sappho and Phao* (2.1.43–89).

96. *ease . . . bulk*] deliver myself of the weightiness of this load. (Metaphor drawn from child–birth.)

100. *laurate god*] god crowned with laurels (i.e. Apollo). A laurel chaplet (which became symbolic of poetic inspiration) was worn by Apollo in memory of his love, Daphne, who was transformed into a laurel bush to escape his pursuit. The story of Daphne and origins of the chaplet are recounted by Ovid (*Met.*, bk i.545ff.).

101–5. Utopiae . . . Utopiae] While the divine powers of the heavens command it, Stesias gives free rein [or puts an end] to his love for the phoenix of Utopia [i.e. Pandora]. The lines are ambiguous, as Stesias points out (106ff.), in that '*solvit amorem*' is capable of contrary meanings. Daniel translates '*Numina caelorum*' as 'heaven's sacred eyes' (p. 383, n.37). For further discussion of the passage, see Bond, iii, p. 558.

105.1. *soberly*] solemnly.

But if it signify 'to withdraw love',
Then is it ill abodement to us both.
But speak, Pandora, while the god inspires.   110
Pandora. *Idaliis prior hic pueris est: aequoris alti*
    pulchrior hec nymphis, et prior Aoniis.
And backward thus, but still all one in sense:
    Aoniis prior, et nymphis hec pulchrior alti
    aequoris est: pueris hic prior Idaliis.   115
He, soberly repeating these also backward and forward, sayeth:
Stesias. Forward and back, these also are alike,
And sense all one, the pointing only changed.
They but import Pandora's praise and mine.
Pandora. Even now beginneth my fury to retire;
And now with Stesias hence will I retire.   120
               Exeunt [PANDORA *and* STESIAS].

ACT. 3, SCENA 2

Enter VENUS [*with* CUPID *and* JOCULUS].

[*Venus.*] Phoebus, away! Thou mak'st her too precise;
    I'll have her witty, quick, and amorous,

111. *alti*] *Corrected in ink from 'alts' in all extant copies of Q.*
112. *hec*] *Q; haec / Daniel (also at l. 114).*
120.1. SD. PANDORA *and* STESIAS] *This ed.*
3.2.0. SCENA] *Q (Scen.);* SCENE *Fairholt.*
0.1. SD. *with* CUPID *and* JOCULUS] *Bond.*
1. SP.] *Fairholt.*

___

109. *ill abodement*] an unpropitious prophecy.
111–12. Idaliis . . . Aoniis] This youth is superior to those of Idalium [a
town in Cyprus sacred to Venus]. This young woman is more beautiful than
the nymphs of the deep sea and superior to the Aonian goddesses [i.e. the
Muses].
117. *pointing*] punctuation.
118. *import*] signify.
119. *fury*] fit of inspired frenzy. Compare *Oth*: 'A sybil . . . / In her
prophetic fury sewed the work' (3.4.72–4).
ACT. 3, SCENA 2] As Bond notes (iii, p. 558), though a change of scene is
marked in *Q* the action is continuous in that Sol remains aloft.
0.1. with CUPID and *JOCULUS*] Bond asserts, 'obviously summoned from
Hor. *Carm.* i.2.33' (iii, p. 558) but see Characters, line 19n.
1. *Phoebus*] an epithet of Apollo, signifying *The Bright* and frequently used
as a substitute for his name.
precise] scrupulously correct in behaviour, proper.
2. *quick*] lively.

Delight in revels, and in banqueting,
Wanton discourses, music, and merry songs.
                                              [SOL *descends.*]
Sol. Bright Cyprian Queen, entreat Pandora fair,   5
        For though, at first, Phoebus envied her looks,
        Yet now doth he admire her glorious hue,
        And swears that neither Daphne in the spring,
        Nor glistering Thetis in her orient robe,
        Nor shamefast Morning, girt in silver clouds,   10
        Are half so lovely as this earthly saint.
Venus. And being so fair, my beams shall make her light,
        For levity is beauty's waiting-maid.
Sol. Make chastity Pandora's waiting-maid,
        For modest thoughts beseems a woman best.   15
Venus. Away with chastity and modest thoughts!
        Quo mihi fortunam, si non conceditur uti?
        Is she not young? Then let her to the world;
        All those are strumpets that are over-chaste.

[handwritten margin note: Conflicting ideas of how women should be]

4.1. SD.] *Bond.*
13. levity] *Fairholt (*levety*);* Lenety *Q;* Leuety *Bond (noting* 'turned u').
17. fortunam] *Bond (*fortunā*); fortuna* / *Q; fortunae* / *Fairholt.*

---

    5. *entreat . . . fair*] use Pandora well.
    6. *envied*] resented.
    8. *Daphne*] See 3.1.100n.
    9. *Thetis*] a sea goddess of outstanding beauty, wooed by both Zeus and Poseidon, but given in marriage to Peleus by whom she became the mother of Achilles. Her 'orient robe' may derive from the Homeric epithet applied to Eos (Morning) evoked in the next line, and may thus be the product of a mental slip on the dramatist's part (see Bond, iii, p. 558). Lyly includes Sol (Phoebus) among her lovers here and at 4.1.254 and 5.1.296–7.
    10. *Morning*] Eos or Aurora, goddess of the dawn, often described as blushing ('shamefast') from her nightly encounters with her husband (Tithonus) or numerous lovers, among whom Lyly includes Sol (see 5.1.296–7). Hence the red tint of the sky at dawn.
    girt] enfolded.
    12–13. *light . . . levity*] The play on the two words supports Fairholt's emendation of *Q* 'Lenety' (though Bond's 'turned letter' is open to doubt). The term 'lenity' is not in itself inappropriate, however, in that a yielding disposition is one Venus might be expected to endorse.
    17.] Why is fortune mine, if I may not use it? (Horace, *Epi.*, 1.5.12: trs. LCL).
    18. *let her . . . world*] allow her to engage in worldly pleasures.
    19–20.] Those who make a fetish of their virtue are strumpets, in that their denial of their lovers is a species of sexual control.

Defying such as keep their company.   20
'Tis not the touching of a woman's hand,
Kissing her lips, hanging about her neck,
A speaking look, no, nor a yielding word,
That men expect. Believe me, Sol, 'tis more,
And were Mars here, he would protest as much.   25
Sol. But what is more than this is worse than nought.
[*Aside*] I dare not stay, lest she infect me too.   *Exit.*
Venus. What, is he gone? Then, light-foot Joculus,
Set me Pandora in a dancing vein.
Joculus. Faith, mother, I will make Pandora blithe,   30
And like a satyr hop upon these plains.   *Exit.*
Venus. Go, Cupid, give her all the golden shafts,
And she will take thee for a forester.
Cupid. I will, and you shall see her straight in love. *Exit.*
                                VENUS *ascendeth.*

---

27. SD. *Aside*] Bond.
34.1. SD. *ascendeth*] *Q; ascends / Daniel.*

---

20. *Defying*] repudiating. Compare *The Maydes Metamorphosis*: 'If it be
false, mine Art I will defie' (Anon.: Bond, iii, 4.1.155).
   21–4.] The position advanced by Venus echoes that of Philautus in a
debate with Euphues over the nature of love (*England*, pp. 293–5). Though
the sexual licence promoted by Venus here is clearly to be condemned, Lyly's
position in relation to the physical aspect of heterosexual love is far more
ambivalent in the earlier work.
   25. *Mars*] Married to the deformed Vulcan, Venus took Mars, god of war,
for her lover.
   protest] assert.
   26.] Sol retorts that for a woman to proceed to the kind of conduct Venus
advocates would be grossly immoral. ('Nought/naught' often carries the
implication of sexual impropriety, as in *R3*, 'He that doth naught with her
(excepting one) / Were best to do it secretly, alone' (1.1.99–100).
   31. *satyr*] a class of sylvan deity, half man, half goat, strongly associated
with sensual pleasures (particularly music and dancing). The term is usually
associated with youthfulness, the older members of the group being known
as Sileni.
   32. *golden shafts*] Cupid was thought to carry shafts of two kinds in his
quiver, some of gold which induced love, and some of lead which repelled
it. Compare Ovid, *Met.*: 'From hys quiver full of shafts two arrowes did he
take / Of sundrie workes: tone [the one] causeth Love, the tother doth it
slake. / That causeth love, is all of golde with point full sharpe and bright, /
That chaseth love is blunt, whose steele with leaden head is dight' (bk
i.565–8).
   34. *straight*] immediately.

Venus. Here, Venus, sit, and with thy influence   35
  Govern Pandora, Nature's miracle.

     Enter PANDORA *and* JOCULUS.

Pandora. Prithee be quiet. Wherefore should I dance?
Joculus. Thus dance the satyrs on the even lawns.
Pandora. Thus, pretty satyr, will Pandora dance.

     [*Enter* CUPID.]

Cupid. And thus will Cupid make her melody. *He shoots.* 40
         [*They dance and sing.*]
Joculus. Were I a man, I could love thee.
Pandora. I am a maiden; wilt thou have me?
Joculus. But Stesias saith you are not.
Pandora. What then? I care not.
Cupid. Nor I.
Joculus.   Nor I.   45
Pandora.   Then merrily
  Farewell my maidenhead,
  These be all the tears I'll shed.
  Turn about and trip it.
Venus. Cupid and Joculus, come leave her now.   50
     Exeunt [CUPID *and* JOCULUS].

36.1. SD.] *Q* (*Ioculus*); *Enter* PANDORA <*with* CUPID> *and* IOCULUS /
Bond; Enter PANDORA, JOCULUS, *and* CUPID / *Daniel.*
39.1. SD.] *This ed.*
40. SD.] *Q; He shoots and they sing / Daniel.*
40.1. SD.] *Bond (subst.).*
41–9] *Not arranged as song in Q.*
46–7] *Line division as Bond; single line in Q.*
46. merrily] *This ed. (following Bond n.); merely Q.*
50.1. SD. CUPID *and* JOCULUS] *Bond.*

---

38. *even*] level.
 39.1. *Enter* CUPID] The entrance of Cupid is not marked in *Q*, and is signalled by both Bond and Daniel at line 36.1. Here the entrance of the sons
of Venus is indicated as sequential, paralleling their exits at lines 31 and 34.
The fact that Cupid speaks of Pandora (cf. 'And thus will Cupid make her
melody', line 40), whereas Joculus speaks directly to her (cf. lines 37–9) supports the contention that he is initially apart from the other two.
 49. *trip it*] dance. Compare Milton, 'L'Allegro': 'Com, and trip it as ye
go / On the light fantastick toe' (lines 33–4).

Pandora. The boys are gone, and I will follow them.
I will not follow them; they are too young.
What honey thoughts are in Pandora's brain?
Hospitis est tepido nocte recepta sinu.
Ah, I envy her! Why was not I so?   55
And so will I be! Where is Iphicles?
Melos? Learchus? Any of the three?
I cure the sick? I study poetry?
I think of honour and of chastity?
No! Love is fitter than Pandora's thoughts,   60
Yet not the love of Stesias alone.
Learchus is as fair as Stesias;
And Melos lovelier than Learchus far.
But, might I choose, I would have Iphicles;
And of them all, Stesias deserves the least.   65
Must I be tied to him? No! I'll be loose, — *Sexual?*
As loose as Helen, for I am as fair.

Enter GUNOPHILUS.

[*Gunophilus.*] Mistress, here be the herbs for my master's
    wound.
Pandora. Pretty Gunophilus, give me the herbs.   70
Where didst thou gather them, my lovely boy?
Gunophilus. Upon Learchus' plain.
Pandora. I fear me Cupid danced upon the plain;
I see his arrowhead upon the leaves.
Gunophilus. And I his golden quiver, and his bow.   75

54. *tepido*] Bond *(p. 559n.); tepedo / Q.*
54. *nocte*]   *Q; necte / Bond.*
54. *sinu*]   Bond *(p. 559n.); sui / Q.*
68. SP.]   *Fairholt (Gun.).*

─────────────────────────────

54.] [She] was welcomed at night by the warm bosom of her guest (trs.
LCL). The line derives from Ovid (*Ars am.*, ii.360).

55. *her*] Helen of Troy. Pandora envies her freedom, in that in the passage
from *Ars am.* just cited she is described as taking advantage of the absence
of her husband (Menelaus) to join her lover in bed. See note to line 67
below.

60. *than*] The sense would seem to require 'for' but it is possible that the
phrase is elliptical: 'love is fitter than [honour and chastity] for Pandora's
thoughts'.

67. *Helen*] Helen of Troy, renowned for her beauty and notorious for
occasioning the Trojan war through her adulterous relationship with Paris.

Pandora. Thou dost dissemble, but I mean good sooth.
    These herbs have wrought some wondrous effect.
    Had they this virtue from thy lily hands?
    Let's see thy hands, my fair Gunophilus.
Gunophilus. It may be they had, for I have not washed them   80
    this many a day.   [*He shows her his hands.*]
Pandora. Such slender fingers hath Jove's Ganymede!
    Gunophilus, I am lovesick for thee.
Gunophilus. Oh, that I were worthy you should be sick for me!
Pandora. I languish for thee, therefore be my love!   85
Gunophilus. Better you languish than I be beaten. Pardon me,
    I dare not love, because of my master.
Pandora. I'll hide thee in a wood, and keep thee close.
Gunophilus. But what if he come a-hunting that way?
Pandora. I'll say thou art a satyr of the woods.   90
Gunophilus. Then I must have horns.
Pandora. Ay, so thou shalt. I'll give thee Stesias' horns.
Gunophilus. Why, he hath none.
Pandora. But he may have shortly.
Gunophilus. Ye say true, and of that condition I am yours.   95

Enter LEARCHUS.

[*Learchus. Aside*] I may not speak of love, for I have vowed
    Ne'er to solicit her, but rest content.
    Therefore only gaze, eyes, to please yourselves,
    Let not my inward sense know what you see,
    Lest that my fancy dote upon her still.   100
    Pandora is divine! But say not so,
    Lest that thy heart hear thee, and break in twain.
    I may not court her. What a hell is this!

81. SD.] *This ed.*
96. SP.] *Fairholt (Lear.).*
96. SD.] *This ed.*
102. twain] *Fairholt (*twaine*);* tawine *Q.*
103. court] *Fairholt;* coutt *Q.*

76. *good sooth*] truly.
90–4.] The exchange indirectly affirms Pandora's readiness to cuckold
Stesias, horns growing from the brow being reputed to be the mark of a
deceived husband. For 'satyr' see 3.2.31n.
95. *of that condition*] on that condition.

Pandora. Gunophilus, I'll have a banquet straight.
   Go thou provide it, and then meet me here.   105
Gunophilus. I will. [*Aside*] But by your leave I'll stay
   awhile.
Learchus. [*To Pandora*] Happy are those that be Pandora's
   guests.
Pandora. Then happy is Learchus; he is my guest.
Learchus. And greater joy do I conceive therein
   Than Tantalus, that feasted with the gods.   110
Gunophilus. Mistress! The banquet –
Pandora. What of the banquet?
Gunophilus. You have bid nobody to it.
Pandora. What's that to you? Go and prepare it.
Gunophilus. [*Aside*] And in the meantime, you will be in love   115
   with him. [*Aloud*] I pray, let me stay – and bid him
   prepare the banquet!
Pandora. Away, ye peasant!
Gunophilus. [*Sourly*] Now she begins to love me!   [*Exit.*]
Pandora. Learchus, had I marked this golden hair,   120

104. Gunophilus] *Fairholt;* Gunopilus *Q.*
106. SD.] *This ed.*
106. awhile] *Fairholt;* a while *Q.*
107. SD.] *This ed.*
115, 116. SD.] *This ed.*
117. banquet] *Fairholt;* bauquet *Q (turned letter).*
119. SD. *Sourly*] *This ed.*
119. SD. *Exit*] *Bond.*

106. Aside] Though no previous edition marks the latter portion of the
line as an aside, it is clear from the exchange between Pandora and Learchus
that follows that Gunophilus is not included in their conversation, and that
it is not meant for his ears. He delays acting on the instructions of his mistress because he is jealous of Learchus and suspicious of her intentions, as
his attempt to thrust himself into the conversation (lines 111–13) indicate.
The similarly surly and resentful tone of lines 115–17 suggests that they too
are spoken aside. From this point onwards the scene becomes increasingly
dense in implied stage directions (e.g. at lines 131 and 133), asides (e.g. at
lines 127 and 153), and private exchanges between pairs of characters (e.g.
at lines 245–50), few of which are signalled in *Q* (see collation notes). The
relatively heavy editorial interventions that follow are designed to assist the
reader to visualize the most intricately plotted scene in the Lylian corpus.

110. Tantalus] King of Phrygia (or Lydia) and son of Zeus, invited by his
father to sit at his table and entrusted by him with his counsels, which he
subsequently betrayed. The comparison is an ominous one, in that Tantalus
was punished in Tartarus for his various crimes by being unable to reach the
food and drink eternally presented to him.

I had not chosen Stesias for my love;
But now –
Learchus. Lovely Pandora, if a shepherd's tears
    May move thee unto ruth, pity my state.
    Make me thy love, though Stesias be thy choice,   125
    And I, instead of love, will honour thee.
Pandora. [*Aside*] Had he not spoke, I should have courted
    him.
    [*To Learchus*] Wilt thou not say Pandora is too light,
    If she take thee instead of Stesias?
Learchus. Rather I'll die than have but such a thought!   130
Pandora. Then, shepherd, this kiss shall be our nuptials.
                                        [*She kisses him.*]
Learchus. This kiss hath made me wealthier than Pan.
Pandora. Then come again. [*She kisses him again.*] Now be
    as great as Jove.
Learchus. Let Stesias never touch these lips again.
Pandora. None but Learchus. Now, sweet love, begone,   135
    Lest Stesias take thee in this amorous vein.
    But go no further than thy bower, my love;
    I'll steal from Stesias and meet thee straight.
Learchus. I will, Pandora, and against thou com'st
    Strew all my bower with flags and water mints.   *Exit.*   140

---

122. now –] *Punctuation as Fairholt;* now. *Q; Bond supplies SD* / *sighs* / *following* – .
127. SD.] *Bond; Daniel encloses the line in round brackets.*
128. SD.] *This ed.*
131.1. SD.] *This ed.*
133. SD.] *This ed.*

---

124. *ruth*] pity.
128. *light*] giddy in her affections, wanton.
132. *Pan*] god of flocks and shepherds. The concept of his wealth derives from the extent of his province, which included all facets of the natural world.
133. *as great as Jove*] The comparison looks back to the previous line in that Jove, as king of the gods, was greater than Pan. Hence Pandora further enriches Learchus by giving him a second kiss.
138. *steal*] slip away.
139. *against thou com'st*] in readiness for your arrival.
140. *flags*] plants with long, sword-like leaves, specifically those of the iris family. The strewing of fresh rushes or flags on the floor of a house signalled the arrival of an honoured guest.
    water mints] mentha acquatica, a Eurasian member of the mint family with scented leaves (hence its use in this context) and whorls of small flowers.

Pandora. A husband? What a foolish word is that!
      Give me a lover; let the husband go!

                Enter MELOS [*and* IPHICLES].

Melos. Oh, Iphicles, behold the heavenly nymph!
Iphicles. We may behold her, but she scorns our love.
Pandora. Are these the shepherds that made love to me?   145
Melos. Yea, and the shepherds that yet love thee still.
Iphicles. Oh, that Pandora would regard my suit!
Pandora. They look like water nymphs, but speak like men.
      Thou [*To Melos*] should be Nature in a man's attire,
      And thou [*To Iphicles*] young Ganymede, minion to Jove.   150
Melos. Then would I make a world, and give it thee.
Iphicles. Then would I leave great Jove to follow thee.
Pandora. [*Aside*] Melos is loveliest, Melos is my love.
      [*To Melos*] Come hither, Melos, I must tell thee news,
      News tragical to thee and to thy flock.   155
                           She whispers in his ear.
      Melos, I love thee. Meet me in the vale.
                           She speaks aloud.
      I saw him in the wolf's mouth, Melos. Fly!
Melos. Oh, that so fair a lamb should be devoured!
      I'll go and rescue him!   [*Exit* MELOS.]
Iphicles. Could Iphicles go from thee for a lamb?   160
      The wolf take all my flock, so I have thee.
      Will me to dive for pearl into the sea,
      To fetch the feathers of the Arabian bird,
      The golden apples from the Hesperian wood,

142.1. SD. *and* IPHICLES] *Fairholt.*
149. SD.] *This ed.*
150. SD.] *This ed.*
153. SD.] *Bond.*
154. SD.] *This ed.*
156.1. SD.] *Q; She speaks aloud again* / *Daniel.*
159. SD.] *Bond.*
164. the Hesperian] *Q;* th'Hesperian *Daniel.*

148. *water nymphs*] Nereids, renowned for their beauty. The fact that
Pandora compares the shepherds to water deities may suggest that they are
in tears. In conjunction with the images that follow the comparison suggests
the effeminacy of the shepherds and the dominant role of Pandora in the
relationships that ensue.

157. *him*] the lamb. See Melos' response in the next line.

Mermaid's glass, Flora's habiliment,   165
So I may have Pandora for my love.
Pandora. [*Aside*] He that would do all this must love me well,
And why should he love me and I not him?
[*To Iphicles*] Wilt thou, for my sake, go into yon
grove?
And we will sing unto the wild birds' notes,   170
And be as pleasant as the western wind,
That kisses flowers and wantons with their leaves.
Iphicles. Will I? Oh, that Pandora would!
Pandora. I will, and therefore follow, Iphicles.
                Exeunt [PANDORA *and* IPHICLES].

         Enter STESIAS *with* GUNOPHILUS.

Stesias. Did base Learchus court my heavenly love?   175
Pardon me, Pan, if to revenge this deed,
I shed the blood of that dissembling swain;
With jealous fire my heart begins to burn.
Ah, bring me where he is, Gunophilus,
Lest he entice Pandora from my bower.   180

165. Mermaid's] *Daniel;* Maremaydes *Q;* The maremaydes' *Fairholt.*
167. SD.] *This ed.*
169. SD.] *This ed.*
170. wild birds'] *This ed.;* wilde birdes *Q;* wilde birde's *Fairholt;* wild birds
Daniel.
174.1. SD. PANDORA *and* IPHICLES] *This ed.*

163–5.] The four tasks proposed here are all but impossible. Rather than
shedding its feathers, the Phoenix ('the Arabian bird') consumed itself in
flames and was reborn from the ashes. The gaining of the golden apples
guarded by the Hesperides and the dragon Ladon was so difficult that it was
one of the labours undertaken by Hercules. The mermaid, frequently represented as looking in her glass, appears to have been associated by Lyly with
the Syren in luring men to destruction (see *Love's Metamorphosis,* 4.2.22–95).
The robe ('habiliment') of flowers worn by Flora as goddess of the spring is
inseparable from her godhead. Iphicles' readiness to undertake these tasks
in order to bring Pandora such rare and valuable gifts is indicative of the
extravagance of his passion. For 'pearl' in the previous line, see 4.1.272n.
    169–70.] Bond notes: 'It is impossible not to recall the song in *As You Like
It* "Under the greenwood tree," with the lines "And turn his merry note Unto
the sweet bird's throat"' (iii, p. 559).
    172. *wantons*] toys, plays wantonly with.
    176. *Pardon me, Pan*] As god of pastoralists, Pan would be expected to be
offended by any violence offered to a shepherd.

Gunophilus. I know not where he is, but here he'll be.
  I must provide the banquet, and be gone.
Stesias. What, will the sheperds banquet with my wife?
  O light Pandora, canst thou be thus false? –
  Tell me, where is this wanton banquet kept,   185
  That I may hurl the dishes at their heads,
  Mingle the wine with blood, and end the feast
  With tragic outcries, like the Theban lord,
  Where fair Hippodamia was espoused?
Gunophilus. Here, in this place, for so she 'pointed me.   190
Stesias. Where might I hide me to behold the same?
Gunophilus. Oh, in this cave, for over this they'll sit.
Stesias. But then I shall not see them when they kiss.
Gunophilus. Yet you may hear what they say. If they kiss, I'll
  halloo.   195
Stesias. But do so, then, my sweet Gunophilus,
  And as a strong wind bursting from the earth,
  So will I rise out of this hollow vault,
  Making the woods shake with my furious words.
Gunophilus. But if they come not at all, or when they come   200
  do use themselves honestly, then come not out, lest you,
  seeming jealous, make her over-hate you.
Stesias. Not for the world, unless I hear thee call.
  Or else their wanton speech provoke me forth.

---

191. behold] *Fairholt;* hehold *Q.*
192.] *Bond supplies SD / Pointing to a trapdoor / following* sit.
197. bursting] *Fairholt;* brusing *Q.*

---

188. *the Theban lord*] Pirithous, whose marriage to Hippodamia was
interrupted by the centaur Eurytion, who carried off the bride, initiating the
celebrated battle between the Centaurs and the Lapithae (see Ovid, *Met.*,
bk xii.236ff.). 'Theban' appears to be a mistake for 'Thessalian'.
  190. *'pointed*] appointed.
  192. *cave*] The reference to the cave as a place of hiding below the bower
in which the banquet takes place is significant in relation to the editorial
history of the play in that it led Bond to the conclusion that the action
demanded a trapdoor, and his interpolation of a number of unwarranted
stage directions relating to its use (see collation notes). For the significance
of this assumption in relation to the provenance of the play, see Introduction, pp. 5–6.
  201. *do use . . . honestly*] behave in a chaste fashion.
  204. *else*] if.

Gunophilus. Well, in, then.   [*Stesias enters the cave.*]   205
Were't not a pretty jest to bury him quick? I warrant it
would be a good while ere she would scratch him out of
his grave with her nails. And yet she might, too, for she
hath digged such vaults in my face that ye may go from
my chin to my eyebrows betwixt the skin and the flesh!   210
Wonder not at it, good people; I can prove there hath
been two or three merchants with me to hire rooms to
lay in wine, but that they do not stand so conveniently as
they would wish – for indeed they are every one too near
my mouth, and I am a great drinker. I had had a quarter's   215
rent beforehand! Well, be it known unto all men that I
have done this to cornute my master, for yet I could never
have opportunity. You would little think my neck is grown
awry with looking back as I have been a-kissing, for fear
he should come. And yet it is a fair example; beware of   220
kissing, brethren! [*Stesias peeps out.*] What, doth the cave
open? Ere she and he have done, he'll pick the lock with
his horn.

205. SD.] *This ed.;* STESIAS *descends through the trap* / *Bond; Exit* STESIAS
/ *Daniel.*
219. awry] *Fairholt;* away *Q.*
221. kissing, brethren] *Fairholt;* kissing brethren *Q, Daniel.*
221. SD.] *This ed.; The trap rises slightly* / *Bond.*

206. *quick*] alive.
209. *vaults*] a humorous exaggeration of the scratches gouged in his face
by Pandora's nails.
211. *Wonder ... people*] a rare instance in Lylian drama of a direct address
to the audience by a character in the main body of the play.
211–16. *I can ... beforehand*] The starting point for the conceit developed
by Gunophilus here is the depth of the 'vaults' (i.e. scratches) dug by
Pandora's nails in his face. The size of these vaults is such that merchants
would have been willing to pay three months' ('a quarter's') rent in advance
to secure them, but their close proximity to Gunophilus' mouth has proved
a deterrent to potential clients ('they do not stand so conveniently as they
would wish') in that he is fond of drink.
217. *cornute*] cuckold.
yet] until now.
220–1. *beware ... brethren*] The exhortation, as Bond notes, is delivered
to the audience in the style of a Puritan preacher (iii, p. 559).
221. SD. *Stesias ... out*] The action is indicated by Gunophilus' exclamation, 'What, doth the cave open?' (lines 221–2) and appears to be
prompted by the mention of kissing.
223. *his horn*] i.e. that popularly deemed to grow on a cuckold's head.

Enter PANDORA.

Pandora. Now have I played with wanton Iphicles,
    Yea, and kept touch with Melos. Both are pleased.   225
    Now, were Learchus here! But stay, methinks
    Here is Gunophilus. I'll go with him.
Gunophilus. [*In a low voice*] Mistress, my master is in this cave,
    Thinking to meet you and Learchus here.
Pandora. [*In the same tone*] What, is he jealous? Come,
    Gunophilus,   230
    In spite of him, I'll kiss thee twenty times!
                                [*She kisses him.*]
Gunophilus. Oh, look how my lips quiver for fear!
Pandora. [*In a louder voice*] Where is my husband? Speak,
    Gunophilus.
Gunophilus. [*Equally loudly*] He is in the woods, and will be
    here anon.
Pandora. [*In a lower voice*] Ay, but he shall not.   235
    [*More loudly*] His fellow swains will meet me in this
    bower,
    Who, for his sake, I mean to entertain.
    If he knew of it, he would meet them here.
    Ah, wheresoe'er he be, safe may he be!
    Thus hold I up my hands to heaven for him,   240
    Thus weep I for my dear love, Stesias!
Gunophilus. When will the shepherds come?
Pandora. Immediately; prepare the banquet straight.
    Meantime, I'll pray that Stesias may be here.
    [*In a lower voice*] Bring Iphicles and Melos with thee, and
    tell them   245

228. SD.] *This ed.; speaking low* / *Bond; Softly* / *Daniel.*
230. SD.] *Bond (subst.); Softly* / *Daniel.*
231.1 SD.] *This ed.*
232.] *Daniel supplies SD* / *Softly* / *following speech prefix.*
233. SD.] *This ed.; louder, for* STESIAS' *ear* / *Bond; Loudly* / *Daniel.*
234. SD.] *This ed.; Loudly* / *Daniel.*
235. SD.] *This ed.; lower* / *Bond; Softly* / *Daniel.*
236. SD.] *This ed.; Louder, as before* / *Bond; Loudly* / *Daniel.*
242. SP. *Gunophilus*] *Fairholt (Gun.); Gano* / *Q.*
245. SD.] *This ed.; Lower again* / *Bond; Softly* / *Daniel.*

Of my husband: *descendit ad inferos.*
Gunophilus. [*In the same tone*] You'll love them, then.
Pandora. [*In the same tone*] No, only thee. Yet let them sit
    with me.
Gunophilus. [*In the same tone*] Content – so you but sit with
    them.   *Exit.*   250

                        Enter LEARCHUS.

Learchus. Why hath Pandora thus deluded me?
Pandora. [*In a low voice*] Learchus, whist! My husband's in
    this cave,
Thinking to take us together here.
Learchus. [*In the same tone*] Shall I slay him, and enjoy
    thee still?
Pandora. [*In the same tone*] No, let him live; but had he
    Argus' eyes,   255
He should not keep me from Learchus' love.
Thus will I hang about Learchus' neck,
And suck out happiness from forth his lips.
Learchus. [*In the same tone*] And this shall be the heaven
    that I'll aim at.

                        Enter GUNOPHILUS.

                [*Pandora, Learchus, and Gunophilus talk
                    out of range of Stesias' hearing.*]
Gunophilus. Sic vos non vobis, sic vos non vobis.   260

247, 248, 249. SD.]   *This ed.; Softly / Daniel.*
252. SP. *Pandora*] *Fairholt (Pan.); Band / Q.*
252, 254, 255. SD.]   *This ed.; Softly / Daniel.*
259. SD.]   *This ed.*
259.1. SD.]   *Q; Bond adds / with glasses, etc. for banquet.*
259.2–3. SD.]   *Daniel (subst.).*

_____

246. descendit ad inferos] he has gone down into the lower regions.
255. *Argus' eyes*] the hundred eyes of Argus. Assigned to guard Io by Hera
(Juno) because he was thought to be all-seeing, Argus was charmed to sleep
by Hermes on the command of Zeus. After his death his eyes were trans-
planted by Hera to the tail of her favourite bird, the peacock.
260. Sic . . . vobis] Thus you [work] not for yourselves, thus you [work]
not for yourselves. The tag is often used in the context of plagiarism, and
originates in the lines attributed to Virgil in Aelius Donatus's *Life*, in which
Virgil attacks the plagiarist Bathyllus through a series of similes beginning
with '*sic vos non vobis*'. The best known simile is addressed to bees: '*sic non
vobis mellificatis, apes*' ('thus [i.e. just as we poets write verses from which

Learchus. What mean'st thou by that?

Gunophilus. Here is a comment upon my words!

           He throws the glass down and breaks it.

Pandora. Wherefore dost thou break the glass?

Gunophilus. I'll answer it. Shall I provide a banquet, and be
    cozened of the best dish? [*To Learchus*] I hope, sir, you   265
    have said grace, and now may I fall to.

         He takes his mistress by the hand and embraceth her.

Learchus. Away, base swain!

Gunophilus. Sir, as base as I am, I'll go for current here!

Learchus. What! Will Pandora be thus light?

Gunophilus. Oh, you stand upon the weight! Well, if she were   270
    twenty grains lighter, I would not refuse her, provided
    always she be not clipped within the ring.

Pandora. Gunophilus, thou art too malapert.

---

265. SD.] *This ed.*
266.1. SD. *embraceth*] *Q (imbraceth); embraces / Daniel.*

---

plagiarists take credit] you make honey, bees, not for yourselves [but greedy
humans]'. Here the phrase suggests that Gunophilus sees others enjoying
the fruit of his endeavours, including not only the banquet but Pandora
herself. The tag was sufficiently well known to be recognized without the
completion of the simile (cf. the modern 'Too many cooks . . .'). The reiter-
ation of the phrase may be designed to suggest Gunophilus' ill-humour.

    264. *answer it*] (*a*) give you an answer (*b*) justify it (*OED* v. I 4b).

    265. *cozened*] cheated.

    267–72. *base swain . . . ring*] The exchange turns upon a series of puns on
aspects of sixteenth-century coinage. Though Gunophilus is only 'base', i.e.
a coin alloyed with less valuable metals than gold or silver (hence a social
inferior), he is 'current' (i.e. has value) in that he is acceptable to Pandora.
Learchus' response, 'Will Pandora be thus light?', literally asks whether she
is capable of being wanton, but Gunophilus, pursuing the coinage metaphor,
takes him to question whether she has the appropriate weight for a coin of
a particular denomination. He asserts that whereas Learchus is concerned
with a precise correlation between weight and value, he will accept Pandora
regardless of her condition – unless her value has been too greatly dimin-
ished by the process of clipping (the trimming of the edges of coins to garner
the valuable metals of which they were made). As Fairholt points out, a coin
was no longer current 'if the clipping took away the outer inscription, or
encroached within the ring which formed the boundary of the letters' (ii, p.
281). Gunophilus' reservation carries a bawdy innuendo, in that to be clipped
(or cracked) in the ring is to have lost one's sexual currency by taking lovers.
For another instance of Lyly playing upon the multiple meanings of a
'cracked crown', see *Midas*, 2.2.23ff.

    273. *malapert*] impudent.

[*Aside to Learchus*] Think nothing, for I cannot shift him
    off.
[*To Gunophilus*] Sirrah, provide the banquet, you are best.   275
Gunophilus. I will, and that incontinently, for indeed I cannot
    abstain.   *Exit.*
Pandora. [*To Learchus*] Here, take thou Melos' favours,
    keep it close,
For he and Iphicles will straight be here.
I love them not. They both importune me,   280
Yet must I make as if I love them both.
Here they come.
[*More loudly*] Welcome, Learchus, to Pandora's feast.

        Enter MELOS *and* IPHICLES.
   [GUNOPHILUS *returns with food for the feast.*]

Melos. [*Aside*] What makes Learchus here?
Iphicles. [*Aside*] Wherefore should Melos banquet with my love?   285
Learchus. [*Aside*] My heart riseth against this Iphicles.
Pandora. Melos, my love! Sit down, sweet Iphicles.
           [*Pandora and Iphicles talk apart.*]
Melos. [*Aside*] She daunts Learchus with a strange aspect.
Learchus. [*Aside*] I like not that she whispers unto him.
Iphicles. [*Aside to Pandora*] I warrant you.   290
Pandora. [*To the company at large*] Here's to the health of
    Stesias, my love.

274. SD.] *Bond.*
274. nothing] *Fairholt;* nothimg *Q.*
275. SD.] *Bond (subst.).*
278. SD.] *This ed.*
283. SD.] *This ed.*
283.2. SD.] *This ed.; Re-enter* GUNOPHILUS *with viands, etc.* / *Bond; Reenter*
GUNOPHILUS / *Daniel (following l. 293).*
284, 285, 286. SD.] *This ed.*
287.1. SD.] *This ed.; Confers with* IPHI. *apart* / *Bond.*
288, 289. SD.] *This ed.*
290. SD.] *Bond (subst.).*
291. SD.] *This ed.; Loudly* / *Daniel.*
291. Here's] *Bond (*Her[e']s*);* hers *Q.*

---

  275. *you are best*] it would be best for you (with an implied threat).
  276. *incontinently*] without delay.
  278. *Melos' favours*] Pandora's willingness to transfer favours (see
2.1.156n.) between lovers is an index of her faithlessness.
  288. *daunts . . . strange*] discourages . . . cold, unfriendly.

Would he were here to welcome you, all three.

Melos. I will go seek him in the busky groves.

Gunophilus. You lose your labour then; he is at his flock.

Pandora. Ay, he weighs more his flock than me.   *She weeps.*   295

Iphicles. Weep not, Pandora, for he loves thee well.

Pandora. And I love him.

Iphicles.   But why is Melos sad?

Melos. [*To Iphicles*] For thee I am sad. Thou hast injured me!

Pandora. [*Aside to Melos*] Knows not Melos I love him?

Iphicles. [*To Melos*] Thou injurest me, and I will be revenged!   300

Pandora. [*Aside to Iphicles*] Hath Iphicles forgot my words?

Gunophilus. [*Aside*] If I should halloo, they were all undone.

Learchus. [*Aside*] They both are jealous, yet mistrust me not.

Iphicles. [*Raising his glass to Melos*] Here, Melos.

Melos.   I pledge thee, Iphicles.

Pandora. [*Aside to Learchus*] Learchus, go; thou know'st my

    mind.   305

Learchus. [*Feigning anger*] Shall I sit here, thus to be made

    a stale?

    [*Aside*] Lovely Pandora means to follow me.

    Farewell this feast! My banquet comes not yet.   *Exit.*

Iphicles. Let him go.

Melos. Pandora, go with me to Stesias!   310

Iphicles. No, rather go with me!

294.] *Daniel supplies SD. / Loudly / (also at lines 295, 296, 297).*

295. SD.] *Q; [Lear.] She weepes. Bond (as dialogue, metrically completing
Pandora's line).*

297.] *Daniel supplies SD / They speak softly again / following him.*

298, 299, 300, 301. SD.] *This ed.*

302, 303. SD.] *Bond.*

304. SD.] *This ed.*

305. SD.] *Bond.*

306. SP.] *Fairholt (Lear.); Ler. / Q.*

306. SD.] *This ed.; aside / Bond.*

307. SD.] *This ed.*

308. banquet] *Fairholt;* bauquet *Q (turned letter).*

---

293. *busky*] bushy, wooded.

295. *weighs*] values.

303. *jealous*] suspicious.

306. *stale*] lover made a target of ridicule for the amusement of others.
Compare *Anatomy*: '"Then I perceive, Lucilla," said he, "that I was made
thy stale and Philautus thy laughing-stock"' (p. 81).

Melos. Away, base Iphicles!
Iphicles. Coward, hand off, or else I'll strike thee down.
Pandora. [*Urgently*] My husband hears you! [*More loudly*]
    Will you strive for wine?
    Give us a fresh cup! I will have ye friends.   315
Melos. I defy thee, Iphicles!
Iphicles. I thee, Melos!
Gunophilus. Both of them are drunk.
Melos. [*To Pandora*] Is this thy love to me?
Pandora. Nay, if you fall out, farewell.   320
    [*Aside*] Now will I go meet Learchus.   *Exit* PANDORA.
Iphicles. I see thy juggling; thou shalt want thy will.
Melos. Follow me, if thou dar'st, and fight it out.
Iphicles. If I dare? Yes, I dare – and will! Come thou!
                    [*Exeunt* MELOS *and* IPHICLES.]
Gunophilus. Halloo! Halloo!   325
                    He [*Stesias*] *riseth out of the cave.*
Stesias. Where is the villain that hath kissed my love?
Gunophilus. Nobody, master.
Stesias. Why strive they, then?
Gunophilus. 'Twas for a cup of wine; they were all drunk.
Stesias. Whither is my wife gone?   330
Gunophilus. To seek you.
Stesias. Ah, Pandora, pardon me, thou art chaste!
    [*To Gunophilus*] Thou mad'st me to suspect her. Take thou
        that!   [*He beats Gunophilus.*]
Gunophilus. Oh, master, I did for good will to you!
Stesias. And I beat thee for good will to her.   335

312. Iphicles] *Fairholt (Iphicles); Iphieles / Q.*
314. SD. *Urgently*] *This ed.; Softly / Daniel.*
314. SD. *More loudly*] *Bond (subst.).*
316.] *Daniel supplies SD / Softly / following speech prefix.*
319. SD.] *Bond.*
320–1.] *Line division as Q; printed by Bond as prose.*
321. SD.] *Bond.*
324.1. SD.] *Bond (subst.).*
325.1. SD. *Stesias*] *Fairholt (who omits / He / from Q SD.).*
325.1. SD. *riseth*] *Q; rises / Daniel.*
332–6.] *Line division as Q; printed by Bond as prose.*
333. SD. *To Gunophilus . . . He beats Gunophilus*] *Both this ed.; Beating*
GUN. / *Bond (following* that*).*

322. *juggling*] trickery.

What hast thou to do betwixt man and wife?

Gunophilus. [*Aside*] Too much with the man, too little with the
wife.

Exeunt [GUNOPHILUS *and* STESIAS].

Finis Actus tertii.

---

337. SD.] *This ed.*
338.1. SD. GUNOPHILUS *and* STESIAS] *Daniel.*
338.2. *Finis Actus tertii*] *Q; not in Daniel.*

338.2.] The end of Act 3.

Act 4

Enter MERCURY.

Mercury. [*To Venus*] Empress of love, give Hermes leave to
    reign.
My course comes next; therefore resign to me.
                         Descend Venus.
Venus. Ascend, thou wingèd pursuivant of Jove.
                           [*Exit* VENUS.]
                        [*Mercury ascends.*]
Mercury. Now shall Pandora be no more in love;
And all these swains that were her favourites   5
Shall understand their mistress hath played false,
And, loathing her, blab all to Stesias.
Now is Pandora in my regiment,
And I will make her false and full of sleights,
Thievish, lying, subtle, eloquent;   10
For these alone belong to Mercury.

    Enter MELOS, LEARCHUS, [*and*] IPHICLES.

SCENA] *Q (Scen.).* SCENE *Fairholt. Bond supplies / with transfer at l. 294 / (possibly an error for l. 292).*
1. SD.] *This ed.*
2.1. SD.] *Q;* VENUS *descends / Daniel.*
3. Jove] *Q (*Iove*); love Fairholt.*
3.1. SD.] *This ed.*
3.2. SD.] *Daniel.*

1. *Hermes*] the Greek equivalent of Mercury.
3. *wingèd . . . Jove*] As pursuivant (i.e. herald) to Jove, Mercury was equipped with winged sandals and a winged hat, which allowed him to travel with the speed of the wind.
5–7. *all these . . . Stesias*] Once again, aspects of behaviour deriving from the influence of the presiding deity (see lines 9–11 below) are extended from Pandora to those around her.
8. *in my regiment*] under my rule. Compare 2.1.5n.
9. *sleights*] deceptions, tricks. The word recurs at 5.1.159.
11. *alone belong*] uniquely appertain.

Iphicles. Unkind Pandora, to delude me thus.
Learchus. Too kind Learchus, that hath loved her thus.
Melos. Too foolish Melos, that yet dotes on her.
Learchus. Black be the ivory of her 'ticing face!   15
Melos. Dimmed be the sunshine of her ravishing eyes!
Iphicles. Fair may her face be! Beautiful her eyes!
Learchus. Oh, Iphicles, abjure her; she is false!
Iphicles. To thee, Learchus, and to Melos false.
Melos. Nay, to us all; too false and full of guile.   20
Learchus. How many thousand kisses gave she me!
        And every kiss mixed with an amorous glance.
Melos. How oft have I leant on her silver breast,
        She singing on her lute, and Melos being the note!
Iphicles. But waking, what sweet pastime have I had!   25
        For love is watchful, and can never sleep.
Melos. But ere I slept –
Learchus.   When I had list –
Iphicles.   What then?
Melos. Cetera quis nescit?
Learchus. Melos prevents me that I should have said.
Iphicles. Blush, Iphicles, and in thy rosy cheeks   30
        Let all the heat that feeds thy heart appear!
Learchus. Droop not, fair Iphicles, for her misdeeds,
        But to revenge it, haste to Stesias.
Melos. Yea, he shall know she is lascivious.
Iphicles. In this complaint I'll join with thee. Let us go.   35
Learchus. Stay – here he comes.

                Enter STESIAS *with* GUNOPHILUS.

Stesias. Oh, Stesias, what a heavenly love hast thou!

---

16. Dimmed ... eyes] *Q; not in Daniel.*
17. SP. *Iphicles*] *Q (Iph.);* MELOS *Daniel.*
25. SP. *Iphicles*] *Fairholt (Iphi.); Iphis / Q.*

---

24. *note*] (*a*) melody (*b*) matter of her song. The line plays on the significance of the name 'Melos' (see Characters, line 7n.).
27. *had list*] desired.
28. Cetera quis nescit?] The rest, who does not know? (Ovid, *Am.*, 1.5.25:
trs. LCL). Lyly uses an English version of the phrase in *England* in Euphues'
warning to Philautus of the dangers of 'fond appetites' (p. 226).
29. *prevents ... said*] anticipates my answer.

A love as chaste as is Apollo's tree,
As modest as a Vestal virgin's eye,
And yet as bright as glow-worms in the night,   40
With which the Morning decks her lover's hair.
Oh, fair Pandora! Blessèd Stesias!
Iphicles. Oh, foul Pandora! Cursèd Stesias!
Stesias. What mean'st thou, Iphicles?
Melos. Ah, is she fair that is lascivious?   45
Or that swain blest that she makes but a stale?
Learchus. He means thy love, unhappy Stesias.
Stesias. My love? No, shepherds, this is but a stale,
To make me hate Pandora, whom I love.
So whispered late the false Gunophilus.   50
Let it suffice that I believe you not.
Iphicles. Love is deaf, blind, and incredulous.
I never hung about Pandora's neck;
She never termed me 'fair', and thee 'black swain'.
Melos. She played not unto Melos in her bower,   55
Nor is his green bower strewed with primrose leaves.
Learchus. I kissed her not, nor did she term me 'love';
Pandora is the love of Stesias.
           [*Exeunt* LEARCHUS, IPHICLES, *and* MELOS.]
Stesias. Sirrah! Bid your mistress come hither.
Gunophilus. I shall, sir.   [*Exit.*]   60
Stesias. 'I never hung about Pandora's neck.'
'She played not unto Melos in her bower.'
'I kissed her not, nor did she term me love.'
These words argue Pandora to be light.

---

54. 'fair' . . . 'black swain'] *Quotation marks this ed.*
57. 'love'] *Quotation marks this ed.*
58.1. SD.] *Bond (subst., following note by Fairholt). Daniel indicates sequential
exits following lines 54, 56 and 58.*
60. SD.] *Bond.*
61, 62, 63.] *Quotation marks supplied by Fairholt.*

---

38. *Apollo's tree*] the laurel (see 3.1.100n.).
39. *Vestal . . . eye*] the glance of one of virgin priestesses of the Roman
goddess of the hearth.
41. *the Morning . . . hair*] See 3.2.10n.
46. *stale*] (*a*) laughing stock (see 3.2.306n.) (*b*) decoy, means of diverting
attention (as at line 48 below).
64. *argue . . . light*] prove . . . unchaste.

She played the wanton with these amorous swains.   65
By all these streams that interlaced these floods,
Which may be venom to her thirsty soul,
I'll be revenged as never shepherd was!
Now foul Pandora! Wicked Stesias!

Enter GUNOPHILUS *and* PANDORA.

Gunophilus. Mistress, 'tis true. I heard them. Venture not.   70
Pandora. Fenced with her tongue, and guarded with her wit,
Thus goeth Pandora unto Stesias.
Stesias. Detested falser, that to Stesias' eyes
Art more infectious than the basilisk!
Pandora. Gunophilus, Pandora is undone!   75
Her love, her joy, her life, hath lost his wits!
Offer a kid in Aesculapius' fane,
That he may cure him lest I die outright!
Gunophilus. [*Aside*] I'll offer it Aesculapius, but he shall not
have him; for when he comes to himself, I must answer   80
it.
Pandora. Go, I say!
Stesias. Stay! I am well; 'tis thou that mak'st me rave;
Thou play'dst the wanton with my fellow swains.
Pandora. Then die, Pandora! Art thou in thy wits,   85

---

71. Fenced] *Fairholt;* Fence *Q.*
74. infectious] *This ed.;* insestious *Q;* infestious *Bond.*
77. Aesculapius'] *Daniel* (Esculapius'); *Esculapias / Q; Esculapius / Bond.*
79. SD.] *Bond.*

---

66. *interlaced*] possibly an error for 'interlace'.
67. *Which . . . venom to*] elliptical ('which may they be venomous to').
69. *foul . . . Wicked*] The adjectives here signal the reversal of Stesias' stance. Whereas formerly he had regarded Pandora as fair and himself as a faithful lover, he now sees her as foul and loathes the wickedness to which her conduct will lead him.
70. *them*] the shepherds (revealing your conduct to Stesias).
Venture not] Don't take this dangerous course.
73. *falser*] deceiver.
74. *basilisk*] fabulous serpent, capable of killing with a glance or with its breath.
75. *undone*] lost, ruined.
77. *Aesculapius' fane*] the temple (fane) of the god of medicine.
80–1. *when . . . it*] when Stesias recovers from the madness Pandora attributes to him, he (Gunophilus) would be held responsible for the loss of the kid.

And call'st me wanton?   *She falls down.*
Gunophilus. Oh, master! What have you done?
Stesias. Divine Pandora, rise and pardon me!
Pandora. I cannot but forgive thee, Stesias.
But by this light, if –   [*Closes her eyes as if swooning.*]   90
Gunophilus. Look how she winks!
Stesias. Oh, stay, my love, I know 'twas their device!
Pandora. He that will win me must have Stesias' shape;
Such golden hair, such alabaster looks.
Wilt thou know why I loved not Jupiter?   95
Because he was unlike my Stesias.
Stesias. Was ever silly shepherd thus abused? [*He raises her.*]
All three affirmed Pandora held them dear.
Pandora. It was to bring me in disgrace with thee,
That they might have some hope I would be theirs;   100
I cannot walk but they importune me.
How many amorous letters have they sent!
What gifts! Yet all in vain. To prove which true,
I'll bear this slander with a patient mind,
Speak them all fair; and ere the sun go down,   105
I'll bring thee where they use to lie in wait,
To rob me of my honour in the groves.
Stesias. Do so, sweet wife, and they shall buy it dear.
I cannot stay; my sheep must to the fold.   *Exit.*
Pandora. Go, Stesias, as simple as a sheep.   110
And now, Pandora, summon all thy wits
To be revenged upon these long-tongued swains. –

90. SD.] *This ed.*
91.] *Bond supplies SD / aside / following speech prefix.*
97. SD.] *This ed.*

91. *Look . . . winks*] directed, in Bond's view, to the audience (iii, p. 560),
but the line could equally well be addressed to Stesias, encouraging his belief
that Pandora has swooned. For *winks*, see 1.1.206.1n.
92. *their device*] a trick on their part.
94. *alabaster looks*] pale features (an index of beauty in the Renaissance).
Compare *R3*: 'their alabaster innocent arms' (4.3.11). Used by sculptors as
a substitute for marble, alabaster is a white, fine-grained variety of gypsum.
97. *silly*] simple.
101.] They solicit me wherever I go.
106. *use*] are accustomed.
108. *buy it dear*] suffer dearly for their conduct.
112. *long-tongued*] talkative.

Gunophilus, bear Iphicles this ring,   [*Giving him a ring*]
Tell him I rave and languish for his love.
Will him to meet me in this mead alone,   115
And swear his fellows have deluded him.
Bear this to Melos [*Giving him a bloody napkin*]; say that
    for his sake
I stabbed myself, and, hadst not thou been near,
I had been dead – but yet I am alive,
Calling for Melos, whom I only love.   120
And to Learchus bear these passionate lines,
                   [*Giving him a paper*]
Which, if he be not flint, will make him come.
Gunophilus. I will, and you shall see how cunningly I'll use
    them. Stay here, and I will send them to you one after
    another, and then use them as your wisdom shall think   125
    good.   *Exit.*
Pandora. That letter did I pen, doubting the worst;
    And dipped the napkin in the lambkin's blood.
    For Iphicles, were he compact of iron,
    My ring is adamant to draw him forth.   130
    Let women learn by me to be revenged.
    I'll make them bite their tongues and eat their words,
    Yea, swear unto my husband all is false.
    My wit is pliant, and invention sharp
    To make these novices that injure me.   135
    Young Iphicles must boast I favoured him!
    Here I protest, as Helen to her love:

113. SD.] *This ed.*
114. languish] *Bond;* language *Q.*
117. SD.] *This ed.; handing a bloody napkin / Bond.*
121.1. SD.] *This ed.*
128. napkin] *Daniel;* Napking *Q.*
135–6] *Bond supplies SD / Aside, as she sees Iphicles approaching / following l.*
135. Daniel supplies / Enter Iphicles at a distance / at the same point.

115. *Will*] Ask.
127. *doubting*] suspecting.
129. *compact*] entirely made.
130. *adamant*] a magnet.
135. *novices*] mere beginners (in this instance, in the art of deception).
Compare *Anatomy:* 'Such is the nature of these novices that think to have
learning without labour and treasure without travail' (p. 43).
136. *must boast*] has the audacity to brag.

Oscula luctanti tantummodo pauca protervus
Abstulit; ulterius nil habet ille mei.
And what's a kiss? Too much for Iphicles!   140

[*Enter* IPHICLES, *with the ring.*]

Iphicles. [*Aside*] Melos is wily, and Learchus false.
Here is Pandora's ring, and she is mine!
It was a stratagem laid for my love.
Oh, foolish Iphicles, what hast thou done?
Must thou betray her unto Stesias?   145
Pandora. [*As if to herself*] Here will I sit till I see Iphicles,
Sighing my breath, out-weeping my heart-blood.
Go, soul, and fly unto my liefest love,
A fairer subject than Elysium!
Iphicles. [*Aside*] Can I hear this? Can I view her? Oh, no!   150
Pandora. [*As if overhearing him*] But I will view thee, my
sweet Iphicles!
Thy looks are physic! Suffer me to gaze,
That for thy sake am thus distempered.
Iphicles. Pale be my looks to witness my amiss.
Pandora. And mine to show my love; lovers are pale.   155
Iphicles. And so is Iphicles.
Pandora. And so Pandora. Let me kiss my love,
And add a better colour to his cheeks. [*She kisses him.*]
Iphicles. Oh, bury all thy anger in this kiss,

---

138. *protervus*] Bond (noting 'turned u'); *proternus* / Q; *protenus* / Fairholt.
140.1. SD.] *This ed;* Enter IPIHICLES / Bond.
141. SD.] *Bond.*
146. SD.] *This ed.; as if alone* / Bond.
150. SD.] *Bond.*
151. SD.] *This ed.*
158. SD.] *This ed.*

138–9.] Kisses only, and few, the wanton took, and those despite my strug-
gles; farther than that, he possesses naught of mine. The lines, spoken by
Helen about her abduction by Theseus, are from Ovid, *Her.*, xvii.29–30 (trs.
LCL).
148. *liefest*] dearest.
149. *Elysium*] paradisiacal location, dwelling place of the blessed after
death.
152. *physic! Suffer*] medicinal. Allow.
153. *distempered*] made ill.
154. *witness my amiss*] testify to my wrong-doing.

And mate me not with uttering my offence!   160
Pandora. Who can be angry with one whom she loves?
   Rather had I to have no thoughts at all
   Than but one ill thought of my Iphicles.
   Go unto Stesias and deny thy words,
   For he hath thrust me from his cabinet,   165
   And as I have done, I will love thee still.
   Delay no time; haste, gentle Iphicles,
   And meet me on Enipeus' sedgy banks.
Iphicles. When shall I meet thee? Tell me, my bright love.
Pandora. At midnight, Iphicles; till then, farewell.   170
Iphicles. Farewell, Pandora! I'll to Stesias.   *Exit.*
Pandora. Thus will I serve them all. Now, Melos, come;
   I'll love thee too – as much as Iphicles!

   Enter MELOS [*with the bloody napkin and some herbs*].

Melos. This is Pandora's blood! Haste, Melos, haste,
   And in her presence lance thy flesh as deep.   175
   Wicked Learchus! Subtle Iphicles!
   You have undone me by your reaching wit!
Pandora. [*As if unaware of his presence*] Gunophilus!
      Where is Gunophilus?
   Give me the knife thou pulled'st from my breast!
   Melos is gone, and left Pandora here.   180
   Witness ye wounds, witness ye silver streams,
   That I am true, to Melos only true,
   And he betrayed me unto Stesias.
Melos. Forgive me, love, it was not I alone;

---

168. Enipeus'] *Daniel; Enepeus / Q;* Enipeus *Bond.*
173.1. SD. *and some herbs*] *This ed.; with the bloody napkin / Bond.*
178. SD.] *This ed.*

---

160. *mate*] confound. (Term drawn from chess.) Lyly plays on the word
in Euphues' false declaration to Philautus of his passion for Livia (*Anatomy,*
p. 58).
   165. *cabinet*] small place of habitation (Onions); i.e. the 'bower' referred
to at 5.1.100 and 114.
   168. *Enipeus' sedgy banks*] The Enipeus, a river in Thessaly, is imagined
here to be in Utopia. The river is mentioned by Ovid (*Met.,* bk i.715) as a
tributary of the Penaeus.
   177. *reaching*] far-reaching (*OED* ppl a. 2b).
   181. *silver streams*] tears. Compare *Gent*: 'silver-shedding tears' (3.1.230).

It was Learchus and false Iphicles.   185
Pandora. 'Tis not Learchus nor that Iphicles
That grieves me, but that Melos is unkind –
Melos, for whom Pandora strained her voice,
Playing with every letter of his name;
Melos, for whom Pandora made this wound;   190
Melos, for whom Pandora now will die!
                    [*She makes as if to kill herself.*]
Melos. Divine Pandora, stay thy desperate hand!
May summer's lightning burn our autumn crop,
The thunder's teeth plough up our fairest groves,
The scorching sunbeams dry up all our springs,   195
And rough winds blast the beauty of our plains,
If Melos love not thee more than his heart!
Pandora. So Melos swears, but 'tis a lover's oath.
Melos. Once guilty, and suspected evermore!
I'll ne'er be guilty more; suspect me not.   200
Pandora. Nor I suspect thee more; mistrust me not.
Learchus never touched Pandora's lips,
Nor Iphicles received a friendly word.
Melos hath all my favours, and for all
Do only this – and I'll be only thine.   205
Go unto Stesias and deny thy words,
And as the sun goes down I'll meet thee here.
Melos. I will, Pandora; and to cure thy wound
Receive these virtuous herbs which I have found.
                    [*Gives herbs to Pandora, and exit.*]
Pandora. A pretty swain, worthy Pandora's love!   210
But I have written to Learchus; ay,

191.1. SD.] *This ed.*
209.1. SD.] *This ed.; Exit* MELOS / *Bond.*
211. ay] *Daniel (*aye*); I Q.*

189.] Compare 4.1.24 for a similar play on the meaning of 'Melos'.

194. *thunder's teeth*] Unlike the accompanying references to the 'summer's lightning', 'scorching sunbeams' and 'rough winds', the image of the 'thunder's teeth' is not a conventional one. The concept may be related to the more familiar 'teeth of the gale' (*OED* tooth sb. III. 4), but no comparable analogy has been traced.

211. *ay*] The use of / I / for both 'I' and 'Ay' in *Q* gives rise to ambiguity in relation to the dominant meaning here. Either Pandora is principally accentuating her determination to cozen Learchus ('ay') or stressing her

And I will keep my promise, though I die –

Enter LEARCHUS *with a letter, and* GUNOPHILUS.

Which is to cozen him, as he did me.

Learchus. [*Reading*] 'Learchus, my love Learchus.' Oh, the
iteration of my name argues her affection! 'Was it my   215
desert? Thine, alas, Pandora.' It was my destiny, to be
credulous to these miscreants.

[*Pandora pretends to write.*]

Gunophilus. Look, look! She is writing to you again.
Pandora. [*As if seeing him*] What, is he come? Then shall my
    tongue declaim;
    Yet am I bashful, and afeard to speak.   220
Learchus. Blush not, Pandora. Who hath made most fault?
Pandora. I that solicit thee, which loves me not.
Learchus. I that betrayed thee, which offended not.
Pandora. Learchus, pardon me!
Learchus. Pandora, pardon me! [*They embrace.*]   225
Gunophilus. [*Aside*] All friends, and so they kissed.
Pandora. I can but smile to think thou wast deceived.
    Learchus, thou must to my husband straight,
    And say that thou art sorry for thy words;
    And in the evening I'll meet thee again,   230
    Under the same grove where we both sat last.
Learchus. I will, Pandora. – But look where he comes!
Pandora. Then give me leave to dissemble.

---

214. SD.] *Fairholt.*
214–17] *Prose arrangement as Bond* / Learchus . . . Learchus, | O . . . affection,
| Was . . . Pandora, | It was . . . miscreants. | *Q. Quotation marks supplied by
Fairholt.*
217.1. SD.] *This ed.*
219. SD.] *This ed.*
225. SD.] *This ed.*
226. SD.] *Bond.*

---

personal agency in effecting his downfall ('I'). Though *Q*'s punctuation
'*Learchus* I', supports the second, the force of the pun is exhibited more effec-
tively by the first. See 5.1.56n. for a similar ambiguity.
    213. *cozen*] cheat, deceive.
    215–16. *Was it . . . desert*] Did I deserve it?
    216–17. *be credulous . . . miscreants*] give credence to these villains.
    222. *which*] who. (See also line 223 below.)

[*Enter* STESIAS.]

[*Loudly*] 'Tis not thy sorrow that can make amends.
Were I a man, thou shouldst repent thy words.   235
Stesias. Learchus, will you stand unto your words?
Learchus. Oh, Stesias, pardon me, 'twas their deceit.
  I am sorry that I injured her.
Stesias. They lay the fault on thee, and thou on them.
  But take thee that!   [*Striking him*]   240
Pandora. Ah Stesias, leave! You shall not fight for me.
  Go, Learchus! I am Stesias's.
Learchus. Art thou?
Gunophilus. [*Aside to Learchus*] No, no, Learchus. She doth
  but say so.   245
Stesias. Out of my ground, Learchus! From my land!
  And from henceforward come not near my lawns!
  Pandora, come. Gunophilus, away!
Pandora. [*Aside to Learchus*] Learchus, meet me straight.
  The time draws nigh.
      [*Exit* PANDORA *after* STESIAS *and* GUNOPHILUS.]
Learchus. The time draws nigh! Oh, that the time were
  now!   250
  I go to meet Pandora at the grove!   *Exit.*

                        Enter MELOS.

Melos. When will the sun go down? Fly, Phoebus, fly!
  Oh, that thy steeds were winged with my swift thoughts!

233.1. SD.] *Bond (following l. 235).*
234. SD.] *Bond (subst.).*
240. SD.] *Fairholt.*
244. SD.] *This ed.*
249. SD.] *Bond (subst.).*
249.1. SD.] *Bond (subst.); Exeunt* PANDORA *and* STESIAS / *Daniel (with*
/ *Exit* GUNOPHILUS / *following l. 248).*

---

  236. *stand . . . words*] maintain what you have said.
  241. *leave*] stop.
  243. *Art thou?*] The naivety of the question confirms that Learchus is
indeed a 'novice' (4.1.135) in the art of deception compared with Pandora.
  247. *lawns*] untilled land.
  252-8.] Bond points to the similarity between these lines and *R&J*,
3.2.1ff., concluding 'Shakespeare to be the borrower' (iii, p. 560). For
Phoebus and Thetis, see 3.2.9n.

Now shouldst thou fall in Thetis' azure arms,
And now would I fall in Pandora's lap.   255

Enter IPHICLES.

Iphicles. Wherefore did Jupiter create the day?
    Sweet is the night, when every creature sleeps.
    Come night, come gentle night. For thee I stay.
Melos. Wherefore doth Iphicles desire the night?
Iphicles. Who's that? Melos? Thy words did make me afeared.   260
    I wish for midnight but to take the wolf
    Which kills my sheep, for which I made a snare.
    Melos, farewell. I must go watch my flocks.
Melos. [*Aside*] And I my love. Here she will meet me
    straight.
                                        Exit IPHICLES.
    See where she comes, hiding her blushing eyes.   265

Enter STESIAS *in woman's apparel.*

My love, Pandora, for whose sake I live,
Hide not thy beauty, which is Melos' sun!
Here is none but us two; lay aside thy veil.
Stesias. Here is Stesias, Melos! You are deceived.
                                        He striketh Melos.
Melos. Pandora hath deceived me! I am undone!   270

260.] *Bond supplies SD / starting / following SP.*
264. SD.] *This ed.*
264.1. SD.] *Q; transposed by Bond and Daniel to following l. 263.*
269.1. SD. striketh] *Q; strikes / Daniel.*

255.1.] Iphicles is presumably on his way to the banks of the Enipeus when
he encounters Melos, who has been instructed to meet Pandora in the same
location in which their previous encounter took place (see 4.1.207).
    260. *Who's that?*] Given that Melos is wishing for the sun to go down at
line 252, and declares at line 254 that it is time for Phoebus to fall into Thetis'
arms, it can be assumed by line 260 that the light is failing. Hence Iphicles'
failure to recognize Melos.
    265. *blushing*] transferred epithet. It is Pandora herself whom he assumes
to be blushing from the fact that 'she' has covered her face.
    265.1. in woman's apparel] One of the relatively few examples on the
Renaissance stage of a male character assuming a female disguise. The device
is anticipated in *Galatea*, in which Cupid seeks to revenge himself on Diana's
followers by disguising himself as a nymph, and deployed by Shakespeare in
MND (Flute) and *MWW* (Falstaff), and by Jonson in *Epicene*. For the instability of gender in Lyly's work, see 2.1.198n.

Stesias. So will not I, sir. I mean simply.

Exit [STESIAS *and* MELOS].

Enter PANDORA *with* GUNOPHILUS.

Pandora. Come, hast thou all his jewels and his pearls?

Gunophilus. Ay, all. But tell me, which way shall we go?

Pandora. Unto the seaside, and take shipping straight.

Gunophilus. Well, I am revenged, at last, of my master. I pray   275
God I may be thus even with all mine enemies, only to
run away with their wives.

Pandora. Gunophilus, for thee I have done this.

Gunophilus. Ay, and for yourself too. I am sure you will not
beg by the way.   280

Pandora. For thee I'll beg, and die, Gunophilus.

Gunophilus. Ay, so I think. The world is so hard that if ye beg
ye may be sure to be starved.

Pandora. I prithee, be not so churlish.

Gunophilus. Oh, this is but mirth. Do you not know *comes*   285
facetus est tanquam vehiculus in via? A merry companion
is as good as a wagon, for you shall be sure to ride, though
ye go afoot.

Pandora. Gunophilus, setting this mirth aside,
Dost thou not love me more than all the world?   290

Gunophilus. Be you as steadfast to me as I'll be to you and
we two will go to the world's end; and yet we cannot, for
the world is round. And seeing 'tis round, let's dance in
the circle. Come, turn about!

271.1. SD. STESIAS *and* MELOS] *This ed.; pursuing him* / *Bond (with exit
of Melos indicated following l. 270); Exeunt* / *Daniel.*
285-8.] *Prose arrangement as Daniel;* O . . . know | *Comes . . . via:* | A merry
. . . Wagon, | For . . . a foote. | *Q. Bond prints Latin material as verse.*

---

271. *I mean simply*] My meaning is very straightforward.

272. *hast thou . . . pearls?*] The question signals a shift from trickery to
theft as a product of Mercury's influence. Pearls were particularly valued in
Renaissance England and could only be worn, under sumptuary law, by
members of the highest social ranks.

285-6. *comes . . . via*] The quotation (translated by Gunophilus) is
attributed by Bond (iii, p. 560) to Publius Syrus (*Sententiae*, 85). Compare
Anatomy: 'a pleasant companion is a bait [refreshment] in a journey' (p. 150).

287. *ride*] macaronic pun on Latin *ridere*, to laugh pleasantly or smile.

293-4. *dance in the circle*] Compare the description of the action of *Sappho
and Phao* as 'this dance of a fairy in a circle' (Epilogue, line 10).

[*They dance.*]

Pandora. When I forsake thee, then heaven itself shall fall.   295
Gunophilus. No, God forbid! Then perhaps we should have
          larks.

                    Exeunt [PANDORA *and* GUNOPHILUS].

              Enter STESIAS [*dressed as a woman*].

Stesias. This is Enipeus' bank. Here she should be.

                    Enter IPHICLES.

Iphicles. What, is it midnight? Time hath been my friend.
          Come, sweet Pandora, all is safe and whist.   300
          Whither flies my love?
Stesias. Follow me, follow me. Here comes Stesias!
Iphicles. She hath betrayed me! Whither shall I fly?
                    He [*Stesias*] *strikes Iphicles.*

294.1. SD.] *Bond.*
297.1. SD. PANDORA *and* GUNOPHILUS] *This ed.*
297.2. SD. *dressed as a woman*] *This ed.; as before / Bond; still disguised / Daniel;
Enter* Stesias, *and* Iphicles / Q *(with the entrance of Iphicles indicated again at
l. 298.1).*
303.1. SD.] *Placement as Q; transposed by Fairholt and Bond to following l. 304.
Bracketed material this ed.;* STESIAS *strikes* IPHICLES / *Daniel.*

295–7. *then heaven . . . larks*] proverbial. Bond cites Heywood's *Prouerbes*,
i, chap. 4, 'When the skie falth we shall have Larkes' (iii, p. 560), but the
OED citation from R. Hilles *Common-pl. Bk* (c. 1530) is slightly closer: 'And
hevyn fell we shall have meny larkys' (lark, sb^1 1c). See also 5.1.24n.
    297.2.] No change of scene is marked in *Q* and the action is continuous
in that Mercury presides throughout. A change of location is indicated,
however, by Stesias' pointed announcement that 'This is Enipeus bank'
(4.1.298), while the inference that the characters are meeting in a place other
than that of their earlier encounters is supported by the instructions given
by Pandora to her lovers earlier in the act. Whereas she asks Melos to meet
her 'here' (4.1.207) and tells Iphicles to wait for her 'Under the same grove
where we both sat last' (4.1.231), she instructs Iphicles to meet her 'on
Enipeus' sedgy banks' (4.1.168).
    298. *Here . . . be*] This is the place where Iphicles expects Pandora to be.
Bond assumes Stesias' knowledge of this private arrangement to be an incon-
sistency on Lyly's part (iii, p. 560), but since Pandora has made her husband
the instrument of her vengeance it may be assumed that she has informed
him of the assignation.
    299.] Bond comments: 'i.e. really, he is before his time' (iii, p. 560), but
Learchus' observation that 'midnight is at hand' (line 305) confirms the late
hour of the night. 'Time' has been Iphicles' 'friend' in that it has passed more
quickly than he feared.
    300. *whist*] hushed, quiet.

Stesias. Either to the river, or else to thy grave.

                                     [*Exit* IPHICLES.]

                Enter LEARCHUS.

Learchus. The evening's past, yea midnight is at hand,   305
    And yet Pandora comes not at the grove.
Stesias. But Stesias is her deputy. He comes,
    And with his sheep hook greets Learchus thus!
                                 He lays about.
Learchus. Pardon me, Stesias! 'Twas Pandora's wiles
    That hath betrayed me. Trust her not; she is false.   310
Stesias. Why dost thou tell me the contrary? [*He strikes*
    again.] Take that!
    She is honest, but thou wouldst seduce her.
    Away from my grove! Out of my land!
    Did I not give thee warning?
    Exit [LEARCHUS *followed by* STESIAS. MERCURY *descends*].

                [*Actus quarti finis.*]

304.1. SD.] *This ed.; Daniel and Bond postpone the exit until the close of the scene. No exit indicated in Q.*
308.1. SD.] *Q; He strikes all around / Daniel.*
311–14.] *Line division as Q. Printed by Bond as prose. Bracketed material this ed.*
314.1. SD.] *Bracketed material this ed.; Exit / Q; Exit [driving them out] / Bond; Exeunt* LEARCHUS, IPHICLES *and* STESIAS; *exit* MERCURY / *Daniel.*
314.2. *Actus quarti finis*] *This ed.*

304.2. Enter *LEARCHUS*] A fresh change of the scene of the action presumably takes place here, signalled by Learchus' announcement that 'Pandora comes not at the grove' (line 306).
308.1. SD. lays about] strikes around him.
311. *the contrary*] things opposite to the truth.
314.1. *MERCURY* descends] The descent of the god is inferred here from the fact that Act 5 opens with the ascent of Luna.
314.2.] The end of Act 4.

Act 5

Enter LUNA.

Luna. Now other planets' influence is done,
    To Cynthia, lowest of the erring stars,
    Is beauteous Pandora given in charge.
    And as I am, so shall Pandora be –
    Newfangled, fickle, slothful, foolish, mad,   5
    In spite of Nature, that envies us all.

    [*She ascends. Enter* GUNOPHILUS *and* PANDORA.]

Gunophilus. Come, come, Pandora, we must make more
    haste,
    Or Stesias will overtake us both.
Pandora. I cannot go no faster; I must rest.
                           [*She sinks down.*]
Gunophilus. We are almost at the seaside; I pray thee, rise!   10
Pandora. Oh, I am faint and weary; let me sleep.
Gunophilus. Pandora, if thou love me, let us go!
Pandora. Why dost thou waken me? I'll remember this!
Gunophilus. What, are you angry with me?

SCENA I] *This ed. (in accordance with headings of previous acts in Q).*
6.1. SD.] *Daniel;* Enter PANDORA *and* GUNOPHILUS / *Bond.*
9.1. SD.] *This ed.; She lies down / Bond.*
10. SP. *Gunophilus*] *Fairholt (Gun.); Gn. / Q (turned letter, prefix usually abbreviated on F1v to Gu.).*

---

    1. *Now*] Now that.
    2. *lowest . . . erring*] in closest proximity to the earth . . . wandering.
    5. *Newfangled*] addicted to novelty. Compare Rosalind's description of a married woman in *AYL*: 'More new-fangled than an ape, more giddy in . . . desires than a monkey' (4.1.144–6).
    9. *no*] any (a common sixteenth-century usage).
    10. *We . . . seaside*] The statement is indicative of a further change of scene from the 'grove' where Stesias encounters Learchus at the end of Act 4.

Pandora. No, with myself for loving such a swain.   15
What fury made me dote upon these looks?
Like winter's picture are his withered cheeks,
His hair as raven's plumes! Ah, touch me not!
His hands are like the fins of some foul fish.
Look how he mows, like to an agèd ape!   20
Over the chain, Jack, or I'll make thee leap!
Gunophilus. What a sudden change is here!
Pandora. Now he swears by his ten bones! Down, I say!
Gunophilus. Did I not tell you I should have larks?

18. raven's] *Fairholt;* rauens *Q;* ravens' *Daniel.*

17–20.] the first indication of Pandora's increasingly disturbed mental
state, rather than an accurate description of Gunophilus' appearance. Melos
describes him at 5.1.152 as a 'youngling', while his youth is confirmed by
Learchus, who refers to him as a 'lad' (5.1.153).
18. *raven's plumes*] Ravens were traditionally regarded as birds of ill omen,
while black hair was not considered a mark of beauty in the Renaissance.
Compare Shakespeare, *Son.*, 130: 'If hairs be wires, black wires grow on her
head' (line 4).
20. *mows*] grimaces.
21. *Over . . . Jack*] an allusion to a trick seemingly common to performing monkeys. Lyly refers in *Pappe* to 'an olde Ape [which] hugges the Vrchin
. . . in his conceipt, as though it should shew vs some new tricks ouer the
chaine' (Bond, iii, p. 412, lines 12–14), while the Stage-Keeper in the Induction to Jonson's *Bartholomew Fair* regrets that the play will not include 'a
juggler with a well-educated ape to come over the chain, for the King of
England, and back again for the Prince, and sit on his arse for the Pope, and
the King of Spain' (E. A. Horsman, ed., lines 17–20). The name 'Jack' may
refer to a specific animal, in that Marston alludes in *The Scourge of Villanie*
(1598, second ed. 1599) to an 'apish' person as 'Old Iack of Parris-garden'
(*Satire* ix; Marston, p. 96), while Lyly mentions 'old Iohn of Paris garden' in
Pappe (Bond, iii, p. 406, line 8). *OED* indicates, however, under 'Jackanapes'
(1a), that Iack Napes (forms: Iac Napes, Iacke Napis, etc.) was a common
name in the sixteenth century for a tame ape or monkey. Paris Garden was
a bull-baiting venue to the south of the Thames.
23. *ten bones*] fingers. The oath appears to be one associated with the
lower classes, in that it is used by Peter, the ill-educated Armourer's servant,
in *2H6* (1.3.191). The use of the oath again echoes *Pappe*, compare: '*Martin*
sweares by his ten bones: nay, I will make him mumpe, mow, and chatter,
like old Iohn of Paris garden before I leaue him' (Bond, iii, p. 406, lines 6–8).
The link between the oath and the performing monkey, together with the
use of the word 'mows' (see line 20 above), suggest that the pamphlet was
running in Lyly's mind at this point.
24.] The question refers back to 4.1.295–7 and was assumed by Bond to
be addressed to the audience (iii, p. 561), though it is clearly heard by
Pandora, as her response at line 25 indicates. Daniel suggests that the refer-

Pandora. Where is the larks? Come, we'll go catch some
    straight!   25
    No, let us go a-fishing with a net!
    With a net? No, an angle is enough.
    An angle? A net? No, none of both.
    I'll wade into the water; water is fair,
    And stroke the fishes underneath the gills.   30
    But first I'll go a-hunting in the wood.
    I like not hunting! Let me have a hawk.
    What wilt thou say, an if I love thee still?
Gunophilus. Anything! What you will!
Pandora. But shall I have a gown of oaken leaves,   35
    A chaplet of red berries, and a fan
    Made of the morning dew to cool my face?
    How often will you kiss me in an hour,
    And where shall we sit till the sun be down?
    For *nocte latent mendae.*   40
Gunophilus. What then?
Pandora. I will not kiss thee till the sun be down.
    Thou art deformed; the night will cover thee.
    We women must be modest in the day;
    Oh, tempt me not until the evening come.   45

---

33. an] *Daniel;* and *Q.*
36. fan] *Fairholt* (fanne*); faune *Q. Bond notes, 'Q turning the* n*'.*
39. we] *Fairholt;* me *Q.*

---

ence to larks may refer to 'Pandora's birdlike flitting around', on the grounds
that 'the use of "lark" to mean a frolic isn't recorded until the nineteenth
century' (p. 384, n.63). It is more likely, however, that Gunophilus is punning
on 'lake' (laike, layke), a frolicsome game or adventure (*OED* sb² 1). The
term 'layke' is defined as a play in 1570 and survives in Northern English
dialects in the sense of frivolity or sport.
    27. angle] fishing rod (*OED* sb. 1).
    33. *an if*] if.
    35-9.] This passage and lines 103-18 below may be indebted to Marlowe's
'The passionate Shepherd to His Love' in terms of their evocation of (and
invitation to) an ideal pastoral world. None of the imagery employed,
however, is directly attributable to the poem.
    36. *chaplet*] an echo of an earlier promise by one of her lovers. (See
1.1.193.)
    40. nocte latent mendae] by night are blemishes hid (Ovid, *Ars am.*,
i.249: trs. LCL).

Gunophilus. Lucretia tota
   Sis licet usque die: Thaida nocte volo.
   Hate me a-days, and love me in the night.
Pandora. Call'st thou me Thais? Go, and love not me.
   I am not Thais! I'll be Lucretia, I;   50
   Give me a knife, and for my chastity,
   I'll die to be canonizèd a saint.
Gunophilus. But you will love me when the sun is down?
Pandora. No, but I will not!
Gunophilus. Did you not promise me?   55
Pandora. Not I; I saw thee not till now.
Gunophilus. Do you see me now?
Pandora. Ay, and loathe thee.
Gunophilus. Belike I was a spirit all this while?
Pandora. A spirit! A spirit! Whither may I fly?   60

        Enter STESIAS.

Stesias. I see Pandora and Gunophilus.
Pandora. And I see Stesias. Welcome, Stesias!
Stesias. Gunophilus, thou hast inveigled her,
   And robbed me of my treasure and my wife.
   I'll strip thee to the skin for this offence,   65
   And put thee in a wood to be devoured

46–8. *Lucretia . . . night] Line division as Bond; Lucretia . . . volo / single line
in Q; Daniel prints all three lines as continuous prose.*
54–7. *No . . . now] Line division as Q. Bond prints as two verse lines divided
between speakers.*
56. *Not I] Daniel; No I Q; Bond notes, 'perh. No, ay!'.*
60.1. *SD.] Q; Bond supplies / in his own attire /.*

46–7.] You may be Lucretia all day: at night, I want Thais. The quotation
is drawn from Martial (*Epigr.*, bk xi.104, 21–2: trs. LCL) and alludes to
polarized examples of female conduct. Lucretia, wife of Collatinus, killed
herself for shame having been raped by Tarquin. The Thais alluded to here
was a celebrated Roman courtesan, rather than the Athenian beauty cred-
ited with encouraging Alexander to burn Persepolis. 'Laida' occurs in many
editions for 'Thais'.
   56. *Not I*] Though Daniel's reading is adopted here (see collation notes),
it is possible that Q 'No' is not a compositorial error. The use of 'I' for both
'I' and 'Ay' in Q leaves open the possibility that the exclamation may be a
further indication of Pandora's mental instability and should read 'No, ay',
in modern English spelling.
   59. *Belike*] perhaps.
   63. *inveigled her*] lured her away (*OED* v 2c).

Of empty tigers, and of hungry wolves.
Nor shall thy sad looks move me unto ruth.
Gunophilus. Pardon me, master, she is lunatic,
    Foolish and frantic, and I followed her   70
    Only to save the goods and bring her back.
    Why, think you I would run away with her?
Pandora. He need not, for I'll run away with him!
    And yet I will go home with Stesias;
    So I shall have a white lamb coloured black,   75
    Two little sparrows, and a spotted fawn.
Stesias. I fear it is too true that he reports.
Gunophilus. Nay, stay a while and you shall see her dance.
Pandora. No, no, I will not dance, but I will sing.
                                            [*Sings.*]
    Stesias hath a white hand,   80
        But his nails are black.
    His fingers are long, and small;
        Shall I make them crack?
            One, two, and three,
            I love him and he loves me.   85
    Beware of the sheep hook.
        I'll tell you one thing;
    If you ask me why I sing,
        I say ye may go look.
Stesias. Pandora, speak; lovest thou Gunophilus?   90

79.1. SD.] *Bond.*
80–5.] *Line division as Bond; Stesias* . . . blacke, | *His* . . . *cracke.* | *One* . . .
me. | *Q.*
80–9.] *Not distinguished as song in Q.*

---

67. *Of*] by.
71. *the goods*] the 'jewels' and 'pearls' (4.1.272) stolen by Pandora and
Gunophilus from Stesias.
75–6.] The lines may constitute a confused recollection of Stesias'
promises at 1.1.186–7.
82–5.] Fairholt comments: 'Lovers' play, testing their love by pulling the
fingers, repeating at each pull, he *loves*, or *loves not*; if the fingers do not
respond by a crack at the joints, the answer is unfavourable, the last attempt
on the series giving the final response' (ii, p. 282). The pulling of fingers to
make them crack as a love test was recorded by Iona and Peter Opie as still
practised by school children in England in the latter half of the twentieth
century (*The Lore and Language of School Children* (Oxford, 1959), p. 328).
89. *ye may go look*] derisive refusal to answer a question (*OED* go v.B
32a).

Pandora. Ay, if he be a fish, for fish is fine.
Sweet Stesias, help me to a whiting-mop.
Stesias. Now I perceive that she is lunatic.
What may I do to bring her to her wits?
Gunophilus. Speak gentle, master, and entreat her fair.   95
Stesias. Pandora, my love Pandora!
Pandora. I'll not be fair! Why call you me your love?
Love is a little boy; so am not I.
Stesias. I will allure her with fair promises,
And when I have her in my leafy bower,   100
Pray to our water nymphs and sylvan gods
To cure her of this piteous lunacy.
Pandora. Give me a running stream in both my hands,
A blue kingfisher and a pebble stone,
And I'll catch butterflies upon the sand,   105
And thou, Gunophilus, shalt clip their wings.
Stesias. I'll give thee streams whose pebble shall be pearl,
Lovebirds whose feathers shall be beaten gold,
Musk-flies with amber berries in their mouths,

91. is] *Q;* are *Fairholt.*
95. speak gentle, master, and] *Daniel;* Speake gentle maister and *Q;* Speake,
gentle maister, and *Fairholt.*
104. kingfisher] *Daniel;* kings fisher *Q;* king's-fisher *Fairholt (also at l. 129).*

---

92. *whiting-mop*] immature white-fleshed fish, abundant in British waters.
The term was also employed as an endearment for a young girl (*OED*
whiting sb. 5), allowing the line to be read as a possibly unconscious invitation by Pandora to Stesias to give her a child.
   95. *Speak . . . and*] The lack of punctuation in *Q* permits two possible
readings. Here (as in Daniel) Gunophilus encourages Stesias to speak gently
to Pandora as a means of bringing her to her senses. The punctuation
adopted by Fairholt and Bond ('Speake, gentle maister, and') diminishes the
force of the advice, turning 'gentle' into an adjective qualifying 'master'.
   98. *Love . . . boy*] The comment looks back to Pandora's encounter with
Cupid in 3.2.
   103–18.] See 5.1.35–9n.
   107. *pearl*] See 4.1.272n.
   108. *Lovebirds*] defined by *OED* as 'diminutive bird of the parrot tribe'
but this is the only instance recorded before 1841. The reference may, in fact,
be to the turtledove, emblematic of enduring love in the early modern period,
but no comparable use of the term has been traced.
   109. *Musk-flies*] not imaginary, as Bond supposed (iii, p. 562) but a dark
green coloured fly, named for its pungent scent (*OED* musk sb. 4f.).
   amber berries] possibly a variant of 'amber-seed', an old name for the seeds
of Abelmoschus moschatus, also called the musk-seed. The association of
ideas may have been triggered by the preceding reference to musk-flies.

Milk-white squirrels, singing popinjays,   110
A boat of deerskins and a fleeting isle,
A sugar cane, and line of twisted silk.
Pandora. Where be all these?
Stesias. I have them in my bower. Come, follow me.
Pandora. Streams with pearl? Birds with golden feathers?   115
Musk-flies and amber berries? White squirrels,
And singing popinjays? A boat of deerskins?
Come, I'll go! I'll go!
                              Exeunt [STESIAS *and* PANDORA].
Gunophilus. I was ne'er in love with her till now. Oh, absolute
Pandora because foolish – for folly is women's perfection!   120
To talk idly, to look wildly, to laugh at every breach and
play with a feather is that would make a Stoic in love, yea,
thou thyself. *O Marce fili, annum iam audientem Cratip-*
pum, idque Athenis. Gravity in a woman is like to a grey
beard upon a breeching boy's chin, which a good school-   125

---

115. pearl] *Q (*pearle*); pearles Bond.
115–18.] *Line division as Q; Bond prints as continuous prose.*
118.1. SD. STESIAS *and* PANDORA] *Bond (subst.).*
121. breach] *Q;* breath *Bond (erroneously? citing 'battered* t *of Q').*
123–4. Marce . . . Athenis] *Bond; Marci . . . Athaenis / Q.*

---

110. *popinjays*] parrots.
111. *fleeting*] wandering.
112. *sugar cane . . . silk*] both luxury items in Renaissance England. Under
sumptuary law, silk could be worn only by those married to knights or those
of higher rank, or by those whose income was in excess of £200 a year.
119. *absolute*] perfect, matchless.
121. *breach*] possibly an error for 'breath', but probably signifying here an
interval or pause. Compare Spenser: 'She made so piteous mone and deare
wayment, / That the hard rocks could scarse from teares refraine, / And all
her sister Nymphes with one consent / Supplide her sobbing breaches with
sad compliment' (*The Faerie Queene,* III.iv.35).
122. *Stoic*] follower of the school of philosophy founded by Zeno which
held that the virtuous mind is indifferent to changes of fortune.
123–4. Marce . . . Athenis] My dear son Marcus, you have now been
studying a full year under Cratippus, and that too in Athens (trs. LCL). The
quotation, from the opening of Cicero's *De officiis,* may suggest that
Gunophilus sees himself as a scholar who has learned from his experience,
or that his comments are to be seen as a lecture on the source of women's
charm. Daniel suggests, however, that it may simply be designed as a general
expression of wonderment (p. 384).
125. *breeching boy's chin*] the chin of a young scholar still subject to the
birch (*OED* vb1.sb. 2b).

master would cause to be clipped, and the wise husband
to be avoided.

> *Enter* MELOS [*with the bloody napkin*] *and the*
> *rest* [IPHICLES *with the ring and* LEARCHUS *with*
> *the letter*].

Melos. Gunophilus, where is thy mistress?
Gunophilus. A-catching a blue kingfisher.
Iphicles. Tell us, where is she?   130
Gunophilus. A-gathering little pebbles.
Learchus. What, dost thou mock us?
Gunophilus. No, but if she were here she would make mows
  at the proudest of you.
Melos. What meanest thou by this?   135
Gunophilus. I mean my mistress is become foolish.
Iphicles. A just reward for one so false as she!
Melos. Such hap betide those that intend us ill!
Learchus. Never were simple shepherds so abused!
Iphicles. Gunophilus, thou hast betrayed us all;   140
  Thou broughtest this ring from her, which made me
    come.
Melos. And thou this bloody napkin unto me.
Learchus. And thou this flattering letter unto me.
                              [*They display the tokens.*]
Gunophilus. Why, I brought you the ring thinking you and she
  should be married together. And being hurt, as she told   145
  me, I had thought she had sent for you as a surgeon.
Learchus. But why broughtest thou me this letter?

127.1–3. SD.] *Bracketed material this ed; Enter* MELOS, IPHICLES *and*
LEARCHUS / *Daniel.*
143.1. SD.] *This ed.*

126–7. *the wise . . . avoided*] The observation depends upon sixteenth-
century assumptions regarding the proper relationship between husband and
wife. A grave wife might be thought of as posing a threat to the presumed
intellectual superiority of the husband.

133. *make mows*] pull faces. Cf. 5.1.20. The response is triggered by the
word 'mock' in the previous line, with Gunophilus playing on the phrase 'to
mock and mow' (i.e. grimace).

137–9.] The self-centred nature of the shepherds' responses is indicative
of their unworthiness as lovers.

138. *hap*] fortune.

Gunophilus. Only to certify you that she was in health, as I
 was at the bringing hereof. And thus, being loath to
 trouble you, I commit you to God. Yours, as his own,   150
 Gunophilus.   *Exit.*
Melos. The wicked youngling flouteth us. Let him go.
Learchus. Immortal Pan, where'er this lad remains,
 Revenge the wrong that he hath done thy swains!
Melos. Oh, that a creature so divine as she,   155
 Whose beauty might enforce the heavens to blush,
 And make fair Nature angry at the heart
 That she hath made her to obscure herself,
 Should be so fickle, and so full of sleights,
 And feigning to love all, love none at all!   160
Iphicles. Had she been constant unto Iphicles,
 I would have clad her in sweet Flora's robes,
 Have set Diana's garland on her head,
 Made her sole mistress of my wanton flock,
 And sing in honour of her deity,   165
 Where now with tears I curse Pandora's name.
Learchus. The springs that smiled to see Pandora's face
 And leaped above the banks to touch her lips,
 The proud plains dancing with Pandora's weight,
 The jocund trees that vailed when she came near   170
 And in the murmur of their whispering leaves
 Did seem to say, 'Pandora is our Queen',
 Witness how fair and beautiful she was,
 But now alone how false and treacherous.
Melos. Here I abjure Pandora, and protest   175
 To live for ever in a single life.

148–51.] *Prose arrangement as Fairholt;* Onely . . . health, | As . . . hereof. | And
. . . God. | Yours . . . *Gunophilus.* | Q *(possibly in imitation of the letter form).*
152. flouteth] *Q;* floutest *Daniel.*
170. vailed] *This ed.;* vald *Q;* val'd *Fairholt;* veiled *Daniel.*
172. 'Pandora . . . Queen'] *Quotation marks supplied by Fairholt.*
176. for ever] *Q* (for euer); forever *Daniel.*

148–51.] a parody of the closing formulae of sixteenth-century letters.
   157–8.] The supposition that Nature might be jealous of her own creation
is again indicative of the limitations of the shepherds' understanding.
Compare their responses at lines 137–9.
   170. *jocund . . . vailed*] joyous . . . bowed.
   174. *alone*] (*a*) singly (*b*) incomparably.

Learchus. The like vow makes Learchus to great Pan.
Iphicles. And Iphicles, though sore against his will.
Learchus. In witness of my vow I rend these lines.
                                    [*He tears the paper.*]
   Oh, thus be my love dispersed into the air!   180
Melos. Here lie the bloody napkin which she sent,
   And with it my affection, and my love.
                              [*He throws down the napkin.*]
Iphicles. Break, break, Pandora's ring, and with it break
   Pandora's love, that almost burst my heart!
                                    [*He breaks the ring.*]

      Enter STESIAS, PANDORA [*running*],
        and GUNOPHILUS.

Stesias. Ah, whither runs my love? Pandora! Stay!   185
   Gentle Pandora, stay! Run not so fast.
Pandora. Shall I not stamp upon the ground? I will!
   Who sayeth Pandora shall not rend her hair?
   Where is the grove that asked me how I did?
   Give me an angle, for the fish will bite.   190
Melos. Look how Pandora raves! Now she is stark mad.
Stesias. For you she raves, that meant to ravish her.
   Help to recover her, or else ye die.
Learchus. May she with raving die! Do what thou dar'st.
Iphicles. She overreached us with deceitful guile,   195
   And Pan, to whom we prayed, hath wrought revenge.
Pandora. I'll have the ocean put into a glass,
   And drink it to the health of Stesias.
   Thy head is full of hedgehogs, Iphicles,

179.1. SD.] *This ed.*
182.1. SD.] *This ed.*
184.1. SD.] *This ed.*
184.2. SD.] *Bracketed material this ed.*
185. love? Pandora! Stay!] *This ed.;* loue *Pandora?* stay, *Q;* love, Pandora?
Stay, *Daniel.*
194. die!] *Fairholt (*dye!*);* dye? *Q;* die? *Daniel.*
199. hedgehogs] *Daniel;* hediockes *Q.*

---

182. *affection*] goodwill (*OED* sb. 6).
189.] See lines 170–2 above.

So, shake them off. Now, let me see thy hand.   200
Look where a blazing star is in this line,
And in the other, two-and-twenty suns!
Stesias. Come, come, Pandora, sleep within my arms.
Pandora. Thine arms are firebrands! Where's Gunophilus?
Go kiss the echo, and bid Love untruss;   205
Go fetch the black goat with the brazen heel,
And tell the bellwether I hear him not.
Not! Not! Not! That you should not come unto me
This night! Not at all, at all, at all.   *Dormit.*
Gunophilus. She is asleep, master; shall I wake her?   210
Stesias. Oh, no, Gunophilus, there let her sleep;
And let us pray that she may be recured.
Learchus. Stesias, thou pitiest her that loves thee not.
Melos. The words we told thee, Stesias, were too true.
Iphicles. Never did Iphicles dissemble yet;   215

202. suns] *Daniel;* sonnes *Q.*
209. SD.] *Q; She sleeps / Daniel.*
210. asleep, master; shall] *Fairholt (*asleepe, mayster; shall*);* a sleepe,
mayster shall *Q;* a sleepe, mayster; shall *Bond;* asleep. Master, shall *Daniel.*

---

200. *Now . . . hand*] a confused return on Pandora's part to her earlier
prophetic powers (here in the form of the art of palmistry). Hence the
'blazing star' she claims to see in one line of Iphicles' hand and the 'two-
and-twenty suns' in another (lines 201 and 202).
205–7.] all injunctions with some element of the fabulous or impossible
and an undercurrent of sexuality. Echo pined away for love of the unre-
sponsive Narcissus until only her voice remained, making it impossible for
her to be kissed. Love in the same line probably refers to Cupid, while the
command to untruss signifies to undress or make ready for bed (literally
undo the points holding up a man's hose) – suggesting that Pandora's mind
is running on her previous sexual encounters. The black goat may refer to
Capricorn, associated with sexual energy, while the bellwether is a castrated
ram, leader of the flock (possibly with reference to Stesias). See *Ham.*,
4.5.21–73, for a comparable instance of sexually laden stage raving.
209. SD. *Dormit*] She sleeps.
212. *recured*] (a) made well (b) recovered.
215–38.] The lines are heavily ironic in that the shepherds condemn
Pandora for her duplicity, while themselves having deceived both Stesias and
one another. Iphicles, who declares that 'Never did Iphicles dissemble yet'
(line 215) was ready to participate in the deception practised at the banquet
and departs to convince Stesias of a fiction at 4.1.171; Learchus who complains of being betrayed when 'meaning simply' (line 227) plots with Pandora
to stage his exit from the banquet (3.2.305ff.); while Melos, who deplores
the stratagem practised upon him (lines 228–31), is engaged in attempting
to deceive all his fellow shepherds when attacked by Stesias (4.1.264ff.).

Believe me, Stesias, she hath been untrue.
Stesias. Yet will you slay me with your slanderous words!
   Did you not all swear for her chastity?
Learchus. It was her subtle wit that made us swear,
   For, Stesias, know she showed love to us all,   220
   And severally sent for us by this swain.
   And unto me he brought such honey lines
   As, overcomed, I flew unto her bower;
   Who, when I came, swore she loved me alone,
   Willing me to deny the words I spoke,   225
   And she at night would meet me in the grove.
   Thus, meaning simply, lo, I was betrayed.
Melos. Gunophilus brought me a bloody cloth,
   Saying for my love she was almost slain;
   And when I came, she used me as this swain,   230
   Protesting love, and 'pointing me this place.
Iphicles. And by this bearer I received a ring,
   And many a loving word that drew me forth.
   Oh, that a woman should dissemble so!
   She then forswore Learchus and this swain,   235
   Saying that Iphicles was only hers,
   Whereat I promised to deny my words,
   And she to meet me at Enipeus' banks.
Stesias. [*To Gunophilus*] Wert thou the messenger unto
      them all?
Gunophilus. I was, and all that they have said is true.   240
   She loved not you, nor them, but me alone.
   How oft hath she run up and down the lawns,
   Calling aloud, 'Where is Gunophilus?'
Stesias. Ah, how my heart swells at these miscreants' words!
Melos. Come, let us leave him in this pensive mood.   245
Learchus. Fret, Stesias, fret, while we dance on the plain.

223. As, overcomed, I] *Daniel;* As ouercomd, I *Q;* As overcom'd, I *Fairholt.*
235. Learchus] *Fairholt (Learchus); Learehus / Q.*
239. SD.] *This ed.*
241. loved] *Daniel;* loue *Q;* lov'd *Fairholt;* loud *Bond.*
243.] *Quotation marks supplied by Fairholt.*
244.] *Bond supplies unwarranted / aside/.*

221. *severally*] separately.
   221, 30, 35. *this swain . . . this swain . . . this swain*] Gunophilus . . .
Learchus . . . Melos.
   227. *meaning simply*] being straightforward in my intentions.

Melos. Such fortune happen to incredulous swains.
Iphicles. Sweet is a single life. Stesias, farewell.
       Exeunt [LEARCHUS, MELOS, *and* IPHICLES].
Stesias. Go, life, fly, soul; go, wretched Stesias!
  Cursed be Utopia for Pandora's sake!   250
  Let wild boars with their tusks plough up my lawns,
  Devouring wolves come shake my tender lambs,
  Drive up my goats unto some steepy rock,
  And let them fall down headlong in the sea.
  She shall not live – nor thou, Gunophilus –   255
  To triumph in poor Stesias' overthrow.
                  [*He makes to kill Pandora.*]

          Enter the seven planets.

Saturn. Stay, shepherd, stay!
Jupiter. Hurt not Pandora, lovely Stesias.
               She awakes and is sober.
Pandora. What means my love to look so pale and wan?
Stesias. For thee, base strumpet, am I pale and wan.   260
Mars. Speak mildly, or I'll make thee, crabbèd swain.
Sol. Take her again, and love her, Stesias.
Stesias. Not for Utopia! No, not for all the world!
Venus. Ah, canst thou frown on her that looks so sweet?
Pandora. Have I offended thee? I'll make amends.   265
Mercury. And what canst thou demand more at her hand?
Stesias. To slay herself, that I may live alone.
Luna. Flint-hearted shepherd, thou deserv'st her not.
Stesias. If thou be Jove, convey her from the earth,
  And punish this Gunophilus, her man.   270

248.1. SD.] *Bracketed material* / *Bond (*subst.*)*.
256.1. SD.] *This ed.*
258.1. SD.] *Q; She awakes and is normal again* / *Daniel*.
261. SP.] *This ed.; Mer.* / *Q (see also l. 283 SP.)*.
268. deserv'st] *Daniel;* deseruest *Q;* deserveth *Fairholt.*
269. Jove] *Q (*Ioue*);* love *Daniel.*

  258.1. sober] rational, sane (*OED* a. 11a).
  261. SP. Mars] *Mer.* (Mercury) in *Q*, but the aggressive tone is indicative
that Mars is the speaker. The error is repeated at line 283 below.
  crabbèd] cantankerous, cross-grained.
  269. *Jove*] Daniel's 'love' (see collation notes) is clearly a misreading,
given Gunophilus' answering appeal (line 271) to Jove (Ioue *Q*).

Gunophilus. O Jove, let this be my punishment, to live still
with Pandora!

Enter NATURE.

Nature. Envious planets, you have done your worst,
    Yet in despite of you Pandora lives;
    And seeing the shepherds have abjured her love,   275
    She shall be placed in one of your seven orbs.
    [*To Gunophilus*] But thou, that hast not served her as I
      willed,
    Vanish into a hawthorn as thou stand'st;
    Ne'er shalt thou wait upon Pandora more.
Exit GUNOPHILUS [*into a thorn bush*].
Saturn. O Nature, place Pandora in my sphere,   280
    For I am old, and she will make me young.
Jupiter. With me, and I will leave the Queen of Heaven.
Mars. With me, and Venus shall no more be mine.
Sol. With me, and I'll forget fair Daphne's love.
Venus. With me, and I'll turn Cupid out of doors.   285
Mercury. With me, and I'll forsake Aglauros' love.

---

277. SD.] *This ed.*
278. hawthorn] *Daniel;* Haythorne *Q.*
279.1. SD.] *Bracketed material this ed.*
283. SP.] *Fairholt; Mer. / Q.*
286. Aglauros'] *Fairholt; Aglauros / Q;* Aglaura's *Daniel.*

---

278. *Vanish . . . hawthorn*] Bond notes: 'Accordingly at the stage-direction
"*Exit Gunophilus*," just below, a bush is thrust forth upon the stage behind
which Gunophilus retires: the bush remains, for Stesias below . . . threatens
to "rend" it' (iii, p. 562). The comment is one of a series of interventions
that impose a staging upon the play for which no contemporary evidence
exists. The hawthorn bush required by the scene might have been on stage
from the start of the act, or revealed (e.g. by the withdrawing of a curtain)
at an appropriate point. *Q* simply directs '*Exit* Gunophilus'.
    as thou stand'st] just at you are at this moment.
    283. SP. Mars] As at line 261, the line is assigned to *Mer.* in *Q*. The ref-
erence to Venus in this instance clearly points to compositorial error.
    286. *Aglauros' love*] The allusion appears to be to one of the three daugh-
ters of Cecrops (Pandrosos, Herse, and Aglauros), whose story is related by
Ovid (*Met.*, bk ii.694–707 and 88off.). It was Herse, however, with whom
Mercury was in love, while Aglauros was turned to stone through her envy
of her sister.

Luna. No, fair Pandora, stay with Cynthia,
　　And I will love thee more than all the rest.
　　Rule thou my star, while I stay in the woods,
　　Or keep with Pluto in the infernal shades.   290
Stesias. Go where thou wilt, so I be rid of thee.
Nature. Speak, my Pandora, where wilt thou be?
Pandora. Not with old Saturn, for he looks like death,
　　Nor yet with Jupiter, lest Juno storm.
　　Nor with thee, Mars, for Venus is thy love,   295
　　Nor with thee, Sol; thou hast two paramours,
　　The sea-born Thetis and the ruddy Morn.
　　Nor with thee, Venus, lest I be in love
　　With blindfold Cupid or young Joculus.
　　Nor with thee, Hermes; thou art full of sleights,   300
　　And when I need thee, Jove will send thee forth.
　　Say, Cynthia, shall Pandora rule thy star?
　　And wilt thou play Diana in the woods,
　　Or Hecate in Pluto's regiment?
Luna. Ay, Pandora.   305
Pandora. [*To Nature*] Fair Nature, let thy handmaid dwell
　　with her,
　　For know that change is my felicity,
　　And fickleness Pandora's proper form.
　　Thou [*To Saturn*] mad'st me sullen first; and thou,
　　　　Jove, proud;
　　Thou [*To Mars*] bloody-minded; he [*Indicating Sol*] a
　　　　Puritan;   310
　　Thou, Venus, mad'st me love all that I saw,
　　And Hermes to deceive all that I love.

---

292. be] *Q;* be [placed] *Bond (justifying interpolation on metrical grounds).*
306. SD.] *This ed.*
309, 310.] *All SDs this ed.*

287–90. *stay with . . . shades*] The resolution depends upon the multiple
personalities of Cynthia: goddess of the Moon (Luna), virgin huntress of the
forest (Diana), and deity of the lower world (Hecate). Pandora becomes
Cynthia's deputy in the first of these roles, allowing her to fulfil her other
obligations.
　290. *keep with Pluto*] stay with the god of the underworld.
　296–7. *thou hast . . . Morn*] See notes to 3.2.9 and 10.
　304. *regiment*] sphere of rule. Compare 2.1.5n. and 4.1.8n.
　308. *proper*] own distinctive, true.

But Cynthia made me idle, mutable,
Forgetful, foolish, fickle, frantic, mad.
These be the humours that content me best, *character*
And therefore will I stay with Cynthia. *of* 315
Nature. And Stesias, since thou set'st so light on her, *women*
Be thou her slave, and follow her in the moon.
Stesias. I'll rather die than bear her company.
Jupiter. Nature will have it so; attend on her.   320
Nature. I'll have thee be her vassal. Murmur not.
Stesias. Then, to revenge me of Gunophilus,
    I'll rend this hawthorn with my furious hands,
    And bear this bush. If e'er she look but back,
    I'll scratch her face that was so false to me!   325
Nature. Now rule, Pandora, in fair Cynthia's stead,
    And make the moon inconstant like thyself.
    Reign thou at women's nuptials, and their birth;
    Let them be mutable in all their loves,
    Fantastical, childish, and foolish in their desires,   330
    Demanding toys,
    And stark mad when they cannot have their will.
    Now follow me, ye wand'ring lights of heaven,
    And grieve not that she is not placed with you.
    All you shall glance at her in your aspects,   335

misogyny

313–14.] *Line division as Bond;* But *Cynthia* . . . forgetfull, | Foolish . . .
madde, | *Q.*
331–2.] *Line division as Bond;* Demaunding . . . madde, | When . . . will. | *Q.*

---

317. *set'st so light*] place such little value.

322. *of*] on.

322–5.] The resolution, as promised in the prologue, provides a novel
explanation for the shadows perceptible on the surface of the moon. See
PROLOGUS, line 3n. for the myths challenged by Lyly's version.

326. *stead*] place.

331–2.] The defective metre of *Q* ('Demaunding toyes: and starke madde
/ When they cannot haue their will') points to some omission from line 331.
The line division adopted here follows Bond, and is based on the metrical
regularity of the reconstructed line 332.

333. *wand'ring . . . heaven*] The planets are described as 'wand'ring' in
that their position in the sky is not fixed. Gk *planates* from which 'planet' is
derived, signifies 'wanderer'.

335. *in your aspects*] from your (changing) position in relation to her in
the heavens.

And in conjuction dwell with her a space.
Stesias. Oh, that they had my room!
Nature. I charge thee, follow her, but hurt her not.

[*Exeunt.*]

FINIS.

338.1. SD.] *Bond.*
338.2. FINIS] *Q; not in Fairholt or Daniel.*

---

336. *conjunction*] period of greatest proximity to another planet (in this instance, the Moon).
337. *had my room*] could take my place.

Index

Page numbers refer to the Introduction and Characters in Order of Appearance; act-scene-line numbers refer to the Commentary; 'n' after a page reference indicates the number of a note on that page. An asterisk (*) preceding an entry indicates that the commentary note in this edition adds materially to the information given in the *OED*. Individual words appearing in various inflected forms are usually grouped under one form; phrases are indexed in the form in which they occur in the text. When a gloss is repeated in the annotations, only the initial occurrence is indexed.

Lightning Source UK Ltd.
Milton Keynes UK
UKHW021449250821
389452UK00016B/330